DEAD SOLDIER

A Story of the Living:
The Memoir of
Sergeant Carmelo Rodriguez

Carmelo Rodriguez

Absolute Author Publishing House
New Orleans, LA

Absolute Author
Publishing House

Publisher: Absolute Author Publishing House
Publishing Editor: Dr. Melissa Caudle
Copy Editor: Huma
Interior Formatter: Dr. Melissa Caudle
Cover Designer: Carmelo Rodriguez
Pictures: From the private collection of Carmelo Rodriguez and used with permission.

LIBRARY OF CONGRESS IN-PUBLICATION-DATA

Dead Soldier a Story of the Living: The Memoir of Sergeant Carmelo Rodriguez/Rodriguez, Carmelo
          p. cm.

Carmelo Rodriguez/*Dead Soldier a Story of the Living: The Memoir of Sergeant Carmelo Rodriguez*

ISBN: 978-1-951028-33-6

1.   Memoir   2. Autobiography

PRINTED IN THE UNITED STATES OF AMERICA

"Life isn't about waiting for the storm to pass; it's about learning how to dance in the rain."-- **Greg Plitt**

One setting Carmelo used for his Vlogs.

TABLE OF CONTENTS

PREFACE

As a military veteran myself, I know the struggles our veterans face every day. As we return home broken and bruised, we stand tall and proud, burying everything inside of us to hide our torment. Through this book, I hope to provide readers a look into the struggles of military veterans who are in war zones and back home. By showing the chilling reality, our veterans face each day, and I hope to initiate a lasting change.

Carmelo alive and well.

One way or another, no matter the outcome or impact, here is my story of bravery and resilience. My story is based on a true series of events; however, the names of all characters, other than myself, have been changed to protect their privacy and their identities.

May you find peace and blessings in your life's journey.

Carmelo Rodriguez

CHAPTER 1

I always wondered what cause there could be for a person to appear in court wearing anything less than business casual attire. I watched defendants, witnesses, and jurors mill about the New York State Superior Court hallways dressed not to impress. Seated on the bench outside a courtroom, clad in a crisply pressed blue suit, I waited patiently to be invited inside. Today was the day of my resurrection. Before I could enter the courtroom, I sat in the corridor, letting wave after wave of impending doom wash over me, trying to erode my resolve and months of preparation.

I sat back against the wall, head down. I looked at my wristwatch. *Still, ten minutes until the hearing.*
The words of my drill sergeant pervaded my thoughts, "If you're ten minutes early, you're on time, if you're on time, you're late."

I'm not sure what being thirty minutes early means, but I was there, anyway.

A stranger's voice broke through my spiraling thoughts and yanked me back to the court hallway, "Hey, man. I've seen you somewhere. Are you famous or something?"

My eyes shot up to see a janitor eyeing me inquisitively. I straightened my posture so I wouldn't look as defeated. His eyes widened in realization once he saw my face.

"Oh, oh. you're..." he paused, unsure how to broach this sensitive subject.

I decided to make it easier for him. "Yes, I am the dead vet."

He smiled warmly or sympathetically, like he wanted to extend his support but did not know what to say. He managed an awkward "all right," then hurried away mopping the floor.

This was the usual reaction, an awkward silence, a benign expression, a figurative pat on the shoulder. I suppose I couldn't blame anyone for that because no one knows how to act around the dead.

My wristwatch beeped, the final alarm signaling that it was time to begin.

I entered the courtroom; the tall wood paneled mahogany walls stood resolute defiant and proud, designed to provide the feeling of security; instead, they made me feel small, I might get lost in the small crowd. My anxiety was palpable and could have filled the room by itself. The initial proceedings came and went during the blink of an eye, and I could barely pay attention during deliberations.

Moments before it was all over, I leaned back in my chair, anticipating the worst outcome possible. I felt like I was back in high school, waiting for the football roster to be posted wondering rather I made the team. I wanted to fast forward through the anxiety and anticipation to know the results.

A bead of sweat grew large enough to form a droplet that ran down my neck and soaked into the damp collar of my shirt. Under the table, I wrung my hands together to help concentrate on the proceeding; it didn't help much. Above the table, I made every attempt to appear calm and collected, but my anxious mind was on overdrive.

One question returned to the forefront of my thoughts, no matter how many times I pushed it down, telling myself I'd answer it later, and despite my best efforts, I could not focus elsewhere. Looking back now, I can say that the entire ordeal would have felt like a work of fiction, had it not happened to me.

How did I get here?

It was the kind of cold November day that begs for blankets instead of shirts. I rubbed my numb hands together to feel some warmth and boarded the train. Traveling home from work always presented unique challenges that only New Yorkers can fully appreciate. Today, our crowded subway was delayed unground, between 36th and 45th Street. Fortunately, claustrophobia was not on my list of irrational fears. I made it home despite the city's best efforts to stop me. As I climbed the stairs out of the subway, fresh frigid air greeted me, and an unearned–wave of triumph washed away the grime and frustration.

On my way into my apartment, I grabbed a stack of letters and coupon booklets from the mailbox and headed to the elevator. I shuffled the mail in my hands sorting the important ones from the useless junk mail. Letters from the Department of Veteran Affairs always caught my attention; today's letter was no exception. A standard size envelope with a solitary piece of paper inside.

My thawing fingers fumbled to open the letter in the elevator, by the time I reached the 4th floor and stepped into my hallway, I had the letter opened and had read the first few lines.

Two steps into the hallway, I froze. Walking would have taken too much concentration, and I needed to focus every ounce I could muster on rereading the first few lines. The rest of the mail that I had tucked under my arm fell to the floor, all of it unimportant at the moment.

I checked the return address on the envelope to make sure I wasn't losing my mind, "Department of Veterans Affairs." Still, out in the hall, I could hear the faintest barking on the other side of my apartment door. My girlfriend's dog eagerly awaited my arrival; her excited barks pulled me back into the hallway, I hurried to get inside. I ruffled the fur on top of her head out a habit as I entered, but my mind was still stuck with the mail from the VA. Even though everything in the apartment was just as I had left it that morning, nothing felt the same.

This has to be a mistake.

I made my way through the apartment, following my regular routine. I emptied the contents of my pockets into the dish by the door, filled the food and water bowls for the cat and dog, and I opened the fridge, pleased to find a beer chilled and waiting for me. Whenever I forgot to replace a cold one, there always seemed to be one chilling, anyway. That's just the kind of woman Diana was, we picked up each other's slack and could always count on each other. Diana was the only person I wanted to talk.

I settled onto the couch and popped the top off my beer and took my phone out to record a video message. I narrated the scene while the camera recorded the contents of the letter. At the end, I flipped the camera toward myself to add a kissy sound and said, "I love you."

We both felt that despite the ease of modern communication, most things were best said while looking someone in the eyes, video messages felt like the best middle ground we could find.

Diana was usually very quick to check her messages. I watched the three haunting dots appear, indicating that she was writing a reply, then they disappeared. I imagined her seated at her desk, re-watching the video and dropping her head to the cheap pressboard tabletop. The dots took a moment to return, eventually replaced by one line of text.

"If this is real, you better call Veterans Affairs."

A second message came through immediately,

"Now!"

My girlfriend had no place for bullshit; that's one of the many things I loved about her. She took life with a pinch of salt and a healthy dose of seriousness. The idea of making the call was just an annoying chore at the time. I let it roll off my back. Another message appeared from her as if confirming my sense of urgency.

"Chinese for dinner tonight?"

I smirked and tapped a short reply, "Sure."

I loved that stuff, healthy or not, and nowhere can you find better Chinese food than in New York City.

As I came to the end of my beer, my thoughts wandered to Diana; she was training to become a First Sergeant in the Air Force, and preparing to take command of a company as their senior enlisted Non-Commissioned Officer. We were in a relatively steady phase of our relationship; I found her optimism, positivity, and take-charge attitude toward life very attractive. She kept me sane and grounded.

It was dark by the time Diana arrived home. I heard her fidget with the door key, which was unusual.

One look at her and I could tell she was nervous; I could see through her, but she could see right through me, too.

"You didn't call the V.A., did you?"

I chuckled, the smell of Chinese food wafted through the apartment.

"I'll call them tomorrow." I sounded as earnest as I possibly could.

She'd heard me say that before, "I'll pick some up this weekend," "I'll get to it next week," or "We'll try tomorrow."

Unimpressed, she looked at me with a stern expression plastered on her face, but I guess she was hungry too because she rolled her eyes, overextending the whites.

"You better."

She kicked off her shoes, and we moved to the living room so we could sit on the couch together while we enjoyed our food. As much as I wanted to avoid the subject of being dead, she couldn't leave it alone. I took my fork and dug into the appetizing box steaming of lo mein. She grabbed the mail from the table and read as she gobbled her fried rice. Her face turned pale when she got to the VA's letter. This was more serious than she thought, and her new expression troubled me. Maybe this was more serious than I thought.

"This is serious and can have serious consequences." She held up the piece of paper with her eyes narrowed.

"I told you I'd call tomorrow." It was not an argument, but I was getting frustrated.

"Do not trivialize this," she always spoke her mind.

However, since leaving the military, I didn't like being told what to do, no matter who did the telling.

I brought lo mein laden fork to my mouth, then dropped it. I had lost my appetite.

"I'll just go take a shower."

The cat and the dog followed me into the bathroom, and I sat on the toilet. I closed the door and searched for an old school blues playlist. The blues always calmed my nerves after a long day; something about the genre always affected me. I settled on John Mayall, and I turned on the shower, hot steam filled the small bathroom. At first, the hot water burned my skin, then shot chills down my arms as my body acclimated to the heat. It was the first time that I felt relaxation since boarding the subway hours earlier.

I heard the door creak open, Diana's arm poked in, dropping off a fresh towel, followed by her voice, "You have the shittiest luck, babe."

She's damn right.

By the time I dried myself off and slipped into my pajamas, Diana was already in bed, reading. When I slid under the covers next to her, I felt her tension melt away. I hadn't realized it, but this letter had been just as distressing to her as it was to me. I kicked myself for not thinking about her earlier.

Before I could come up with the right words, she had them. "I love you. I don't want anything bad to happen to you." She offered her cool perspective and a warm hand.

I took both eagerly, thankful to have such a strong caring partner in my life. "I'll call first thing in the morning, I promise."

I kissed her goodnight and rolled over, she left a light on to finish her reading, but as I drifted off to sleep, I noted that I never heard her turn a page, I don't know it for a fact, but I don't think she did any reading that night.

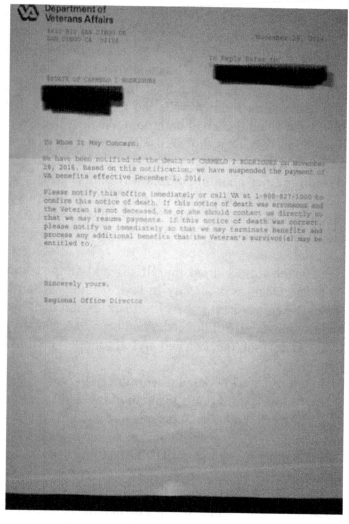

One of the many letters Carmelo received.

Several hours later, I found sleep hard to come by, so I carefully slipped out of bed and picked up the letter. Holding it in my hands, I reread it, and again, each time it brought with it a surge of anger, shattering my defenses. In the safety of my living room, I let myself be angry.

The Department of Veterans Affairs (hereafter, VA) had declared veteran Sergeant Carmelo Rodriguez dead.

I am Carmelo Rodriguez, the living and breathing veteran but a dead man in the VA records.

After several re-readings, my anger reached a fever pitch, and a hot fury shot through me. I crumpled the piece of paper and threw it as far as I could, only to hear the cat batting it around on the kitchen floor. I pictured Diana's face, staring at me after reading the notification like I was a corpse indulging in lo mein alongside her.

With the benefit of time, I now understand her concerns and her insistence on making the call as soon as possible. Sometime between zero dark thirty and my morning alarm, I walked to the kitchen to get another chilled beer, an attempt to calm myself down. I kept telling myself this paper meant nothing; it was a mistake that the VA would rectify as quickly as they could. All my life I trained for the worst of the worst; this little clerical error, probably just a typo somewhere, was going to be nothing but a minor annoyance. After the beer, I headed back to bed to get a few extra hours of rest.

Today was my day off. The last thing I wanted to do was spend it traversing phone menus with the Department of Veteran Affairs.

I woke up and checked the time on my phone. It was now 9:00 a.m. I had forgotten that I turned off my alarm on the days I didn't work. After years of waking up before the sun, I still enjoyed sleeping in when I could.

My phone told me that I had two missed notifications from Diana. That was unusual; she was anxious about the call.

I called her to listen to her complaints about the morning and how tired she was, which was a ritual of ours. She'd vent; I listened, it beat morning talk radio.

As soon as she broached the subject of the letter, I felt my heart jump to my throat. At once, I wanted nothing more than to strike this item off my to-do list.

"Hey babe, let me let you go so I can call the VA right now." I had to stop her train of negative thoughts.

"Oh my god, yes. But you better tell me everything that happens."

"Who else am I going to tell?" Her laughter perked up my mood.

I got off the phone with her, scratched my cat's head for a few seconds, and then went to the bathroom to brush my teeth. I made my morning protein shake, which consisted of thirty grams of protein per scoop, plus a banana -- my staple breakfast.

Then I quit stalling as Diana's voice echoed in as expected, I was on hold forever, precisely the reason why I did not want to make this call. I should have called before I went to sleep, then perhaps I'd get someone on the line by morning. I snorted over my foolish musing. I clicked on the news and lowered the volume to practically nothing while I navigated the push button menus.

The automated service could drive anyone crazy, and considering the sensitivity of my case, I was losing my patience. Finally, an exhausted sounding customer service representative crackled to life on the line.

"How can I help you, sir?"

An important point of training for the VA is only to put tired, overworked, underpaid, and underappreciated personnel on the phones. For the last hour, I had been practicing my answer, but her unenthusiastic business first tone threw me off.

"Uh... Hi. So, just yesterday, I received a declaration of my death from the Department of Veterans Affairs in the mail."

There was an uncomfortable silence on the line; apparently, Customer Service representatives weren't trained to resolve the issues of a dead man. It almost took a minute for her to regain her composure.

"Sir... I will have to have someone call you regarding your case," there it was, the dreaded 'call you soon' response.

"I've been waiting on the phone for about an hour to speak to someone who can help me," I said. "And now I have to wait for a callback?" My voice was a notch higher this time.

She apologized, telling me that she understood my frustration.

"We are just customer service representatives. We don't handle these types of problems. All I can do is direct you to someone in the fraud or legal department."

"How long would that take?" I kept knocking my knuckles on the wooden table, somehow to rein in my frustration.

"If you don't receive a call by the end of the day today, call us back tomorrow. I will document this conversation so the rep who calls you will understand the case." Before she hung up, her training takes over, "Is there anything else I can help you with?"

I think about it for a moment, if this is real, is there anything she can do? What about my benefits? Insurance? This might be more serious than I thought. I answer, "No!"

and hang up, my training took over, spending as little time on the phone with the VA as possible.

I sat on my couch, thinking about the unfruitful call to VA. One thing was sure I would not let my life stop. My life had been a series of problems and solutions one after another, the last one fading from memory just in time to usher in the next and I wouldn't let this get the best of me.

I changed into my gym clothes and headed to the door. I needed to sweat this out. As I entered the elevator, I couldn't shake the feeling of forgetting something. Instinctively I checked my phone for a clue. An email notification propelled a memory into the forefront of my mind; I had been waiting on the results of an exam! I logged into my mailing account to check if the results were out.

Enrolling in the MBA program was one of the best decisions in my life. I heaved a sigh of relief as the results from the last assessments weren't revealed, yet. I couldn't afford anything lower than a B as that would jeopardize my continuing education. A mistaken mail from the VA would not hamper the life I had built after going through so much. I was determined.

CHAPTER 2

My name is Carmelo Rodriguez, The first and only son born to Linda and Michael Rodriguez. My life should have been sorted; however, I am the result of a toxic relationship, born as a liability, and brought up in a neglectful home by a broken Family.

With a mostly absentee mother and a convicted felon of a father, he was sentenced to twenty years, growing up, life wasn't easy bouncing between homeless shelters, repeat visits from child services, and mountains of emotional and verbal abuse, I survived.

As an emotionally volatile teenager, who had never had any direction or support, I struggled to find a path for my life. Miraculously, through my several brushes with law enforcement, I managed to stay out of jail. Maybe the officers I interacted with took pity on me or maybe, like my parents, I simply wasn't worth their time.

When I turned eighteen, I was desperate to find my place in the world. When the invitation to my higher calling came from a source that I had never expected, I jumped on it.

"Would you like to be part of the action? Would you like to be part of the elite? Join our combat forces. I think that the 19D Cavalry scout would be perfect for you. From there, you can attend Ranger school and ultimately join Special Forces. What do you think? Do you think you have what it takes?"

The U.S. Army Recruiter's invitation to belong was like a golden ticket for my immature eighteen-year-old mind. I knew that I didn't want a... I'm sorry to admit that I thought like this, but a 'boring' job in a factory or an office. Being a part of the Army's heraldic Cavalry history held great appeal, so, like so many aimless teenagers before me, in the summer of 2005, I signed my life over to the U.S. Army for a term of not less than four years.

I honestly thought basic training would be harder than it turned out to be. Despite their best efforts, the drill sergeants didn't bother me much. All they could do was to yell, and they shouted all the time. Thanks to my parents, I was utterly impervious on the flip side. The drill sergeants who were calm and patient always left a positive impact on me, given I had no such leadership all my life.

I have since learned that children need structure to grow and mature; my emotional development lacked these disciplines. The structure that I found in basic training finally showed me how orderly and structured life could be. I leaned into 'the suck,' as some call it, and found that I liked contributing to something bigger than myself. A military unit, like a family, is bigger than the sum of its parts and where one of the parts may lack, another can make up for it, this is unit cohesion at its finest. It's a shame it took eighteen years to learn this lesson.

As the training began, my greatest struggle was on the firing line. In Basic Rifle Marksmanship, (BFM), I had to contend with different problems, which meant I was always the last one to qualify. My glasses would fog, or sweat would run into my eyes, rendering me almost blind. Every time I was called to send rounds downrange, it seemed I was cursed. What did not help was that no one leaves the range until every soldier had completed their qualification for BFM. Each attempt, the mounting pressure from my comrades, would throw my concentration.

And then there was the food...

There was just so much food, something I wasn't accustomed to after growing up and never knowing what a well-stocked pantry looked like as a child. As a kid, I was practically malnourished, and the Army life and eating forced me to gain twenty-five pounds in the six months to carry me through the rigorous physical training. I needed all the energy I could stomach, since running in the Army was not as simple as going out for a jog. We had to carry seventy-five-pound rucksacks on our backs and humped (climbed) through more ankle-twisting sand, rocks, and mud.

Those grueling rucksack marches were designed to be difficult; they were meant to weed out all the guys who weren't mentally tough enough to make it through basic training. The drill sergeants know that muscles could be built, but a determination was not as readily available in a soldier. The idea of quitting creeps into every soldier's mind now and then, and on one exceptionally long march, near the end of my training, I nearly succumbed like so many before did.

During the final rucksack march, after passing a few appropriately named landmarks such as Heartbreak Hill, right into Cry Baby Mountain, it seemed that everything on Fort Benning had a hill named after something or someone, hill after never-ending hill. At one point, during this march, I realized the guys behind me started disappearing. On every march, a deuce and a half, big troop-carrying truck, picked up the injured and quitters, as the truck of the dropouts crept up, right behind me. I tried picking up my pace to outrun the truck.

"Get in the truck, Rodriguez," the drill sergeant barked from the comfort of the driver's seat.

I was not ready to listen to him; so, I just kept running without slowing.

"Get in the fucking truck Hot Rod," he called my nickname.

I kept running, blocking his voice through the haze of pain, clouding my mind.

"You don't have what it takes." His verbal assaults on my will power meant to strip me of my resolve. I was determined to block him out and kept my feet moving. I had to keep moving, no matter what; to stop meant to fail, to slow meant to fail, to give any substance to his taunts, would negate all the gains and ground I had covered, not only in the last several hours but also several months of training.

"Get in the fucking truck, or I will put you into it!" He was shouting in my ear now, but I knew it was a trick. No one orders you to fail, and I would not fail the test.

Tears filled my eyes, and with my heart pounding with rage, I bore my eyes into his and shouted back with all the strength left in my body, "Fuck you drill sergeant!"

All the instructors immediately surrounded me.

"What the fuck did you just say?"

16

"I said, fuck you drill sergeant. I'm not getting in that fucking truck." My panting somewhat undercut the power of my statement, but I still got the point across.

"I didn't come all this way to end up with all the other fucking quitters in the back of the truck. If I'm going to get dropped, let me do this as a soldier should." The dread of quitting the single institution that gave my life meaning, filled me with strange confidence that allowed me to defy my instructors, and push through the pain. I knew only one thing in that moment of fear and pain, and that they would need to drag my cold body off the course before I would drop my pack and mount the truck.

"You think you got what it takes?" the first sergeant, the most senior instructor in the cadre, yelled the same question that my recruiter posed to me when I signed up six months ago.

My answer hadn't changed; instead, I had a stubborn determination and resolve.

"Yes, First Sergeant," I said.

"Good! Now double-time your ass to the front of the formation."

I could see a glint in his eyes as he recognized the resolve in my spirit.

Five more miles.

"HOOAH First Sergeant," I yelled at the top of my lungs to re-energize my tired and bruised body. I quickened my pace, one foot in front of the other, desperate to reach the front of the formation. My mind more than willing to complete the task; my body, however, had other plans. I fell flat on the ground crushed under the heavyweight of the gear, the precious breath knocked from my lungs. I pushed against the asphalt near the top of Sand Hill trying to get my aching legs beneath me; every muscle screamed, *stay down.*

Like a boxer fighting to remain conscious and climb off the canvas, the drill sergeants saw that I still had fight left in me, had they seen otherwise, a fall like mine would have been a forced quit, and a ticket to the back of the quitter's truck.

Instead of a ten count, the sound in my ears was, "Hot Rod, Hot Rod, Hot Rod!" My fellow trainees pumped their fists in the air, urging me to get up.

They too sensed my determination, and when someone won't quit on you, you don't quit on them. They continued chanting until I managed to rise. In a gesture of true brotherhood, two soldiers broke from the formation and circled around behind me, they opened up my ruck and took some of my gear, distributing among the platoon. Their grand gesture made me feel like I was born again. For the first time in my life, I thought I was finally where I belonged.

When I found out what they took from my bag, it only amounted to about five pounds of gear, which may not sound like much, but ounces make pounds, and a pound makes a difference. Maybe it was the symbolic gesture of the platoon lightening my load and not the actual poundage, but when they slapped the back of my helmet and said, "Let's step it out," I ran like I never had in my life; I felt like a new man. I fixed my eyes on the next hill's peak and ran like my life depended on getting there. By the time we crossed the finish line, I was leading the charge, the platoon running in step behind me -- we finished together, a victory earned only by those who refused to give up.

My basic training graduation ceremony remains, to this day, one of my proudest moments. My Commander and First Sergeant handed out the National Defense Service medal to all the graduates, an award that says you are a member of the military who had completed basic training, an automatic 'gimme' award. Being that a ceremony in the Army must look crisp and polished, my position in the formation, as the shortest soldier in my platoon, was in the rear, and I was last to receive my medal.

My commander spoke candidly, "You shouldn't get this, but I have spoken with all of your instructors and the First Sergeant. We think you have what it takes to join the team." He chuckled, pleased with himself, "You've got the biggest balls I've seen on a little man in a long time."

Next, my First Sergeant, instead of mincing words, maybe because he wanted to get out of the Georgia sun beating down on the parade field, punched my shoulder and said, "Fuck him. I'd take you into combat any day. I'll see you out there, Private."

After eighteen years of being kicked around and beaten down, I had a place and a direction. The Army had done what no one, not even my parents had done, accepted me despite my flaws. I felt at home.

***

It had been several days, but there was no update from the Department of Veterans Affairs, and I was starting to worry. Calling them back did not help; the representatives always had their canned response ready, to wait for a callback. So I went about as normal as possible living my life as a dead man.

It was freezing in mid-November in New York; I was grateful my apartment building had a gym in the basement, a luxury afforded to few in the city.

I eagerly poured two heaping scoops of a new pre-workout supplement into a shaker cup with some cold water, hoping the new drink would give me gratuitous amounts of energy. Before the jitters set in, I pictured Diana frowning.

"You should use these drinks in moderation, babe," she'd always grimace at my fixation with these shakes and power drinks.

What can I say? I'm a man of many shakes. The thought of my adorable girlfriend brought a smile to my face. As I chugged the drink, I grabbed my headphones and keys and headed to the gym.

The gym in the building was referred to as a man's gym since there was nothing fancy about it. There were only weights and solid steel plates, but that was all I needed. The benches had been worn down by weight lifting savages over the years. The wretched gym that Diana refused even to walk past had the typical musty, sweaty smell that I have grown to love despite the lack of equipment and subpar facilities. I still loved hitting up this musty and humid muscle mecca to burn off the calories. Years away from military service have not changed my fitness routine; weight training made me feel in control of any situation.

I did my usual thirty minutes on the Stairmaster, to start things off with a light coat of sweat, and then started a rigorous back workout. I was busy lifting when I heard my cell phone ring; somebody was calling from California. The horrible reception in the basement made answering the call impossible, but I had a feeling this was from the VA. I groaned, thinking I'd have to rerun the one-eight-hundred gauntlet to get them to call me back. I cursed at my phone and wrapped up my work out. To make up for the missed weight training, I took the stairs back to my apartment, which I began to regret around floor three.

It must have been my lucky day since the phone rang somewhere between floors seven and ten, and it was from the same number. I answered.

"Good afternoon, this is Jim Todd, an attorney from the Department of Veterans Affairs. Am I talking to Carmelo Rodriguez?"

This whole time I had been expecting a customer service supervisor, not anyone I would have considered being the "big guns."

Jim bombarded me with a line of questions to verify my identity and to ensure that I was, in fact, not dead. After a moment or two, he concluded that I was indeed alive and asked me to visit the Veterans Affairs Regional Office in Manhattan, New York, to "fix my paperwork." This oversimplification of the problem made me feel like this whole ordeal was somehow my fault. He also asked me to bring the letter and any other documents that I had received.

"Umm... I have received nothing else."

Although he said it was fine, I wondered what else might head my way, or what else I would have received had I been 'alive.' Why would they send correspondence to a dead man? "Thanks for your help, Jim."

I ended the call and quickly dragged my laptop from across the table. I had to research my unique case while I wondered why I didn't do it earlier. Although I knew better than to rely on *Google*, it never gave good news. Well, *Google* did not disappoint at all. As I typed in "Veteran declared dead by the VA," I was blown away by how frequently this happened. There were cases upon cases of veterans erroneously; in fact, there were four-thousand two hundred cases just like mine in the last five years.

"Ho... lee... shit!" I said out loud while scrolling past article after article.

I sent a video message to Diana summarizing my online research and attached the link so she could analyze the results herself. Work was busy for her, but she loved having an excuse to do something else.

I spent hours online trying to find some resolution or a positive outcome from this whole "dead man" problem -- there were no happy endings.

Our barking dog snapped me out of my deep *Google* coma. Before I could bark back my usual, "Shush!" something hit the front door. Mail carriers often don't even break stride while dropping off packages in New York. I went to the door to check, and sure enough, there was a package addressed to Diana at my feet. I looked down the hallway just in time to catch the last glimpse of the mailman disappearing around the corner. I shouted a half-sincere half-sarcastic, "Thank you!"

Diana's package reminded me that Jim, the VA attorney, implied that I might receive something important about my situation. With my foot, I nudged the package through the door and made my way downstairs, opting to take the elevator this time to check the mailbox.

Back in the elevator, I sifted through the mail, newsletter, red book, bill, bill, bill... Department of the Treasury. This can't be good. I tear it open to find a check for $300; the memo line read, "Funeral expenses."

I sighed, knowing in my gut that this was not going to be as simple as going to the VA and fixing my paperwork. I needed to settle in for a long road ahead.

CHAPTER 3

My High Mobility Multipurpose Wheeled Vehicle, Humvee, for short, cruised down the deserted stretch of Iraqi highway, topping out at about fifty miles per hour, the V-8 turbo engine competing with the reinforced armor and the fully kitted soldiers inside drastically weighed down the eight-ton war machine. I rode in the passenger seat, scanning the road ahead, careful not to daze out watching the Humvee ahead of us. The lead vehicle, the one fifty meters ahead of us passed an unremarkable patch of road, that to me would have been like the thousands of patches before, but when my vehicle rolled over it, we were hit with the full force of a buried 155-shell, the largest artillery round in the US arsenal.

The Improvised Explosive Device, IED, detonated on the right side of my vehicle, rocking the truck violently, filling the cab with smoke and debris. When I regained my senses a moment later, all I heard was a deafening ring. Beyond dazed, I look down at my hands; they were still attached. *Thank God for small miracles.* I followed my arms and started touching myself to check for bleeding. Training really does take over in moments of shock. My self-assessment showed no major holes and nothing missing. I felt a warm sensation trickling down my neck; and discovered blood running from my ears. I shrugged it off. *If there's something wrong with my brain, there's not much I can do about it.*

I turned my attention to the rest of the crew. First, I looked for my driver, thank God he was still there, in relatively one piece, one hand on the wheel, the other in the middle of his injury assessment, he too had blood leaking from his ears, and his right eye didn't look good. His lips were moving, but I could not for the life of me, figure out what he was saying, maybe... "Odd! Odd!"

I didn't think it too strange that a roadside bomb had detonated, and we were still alive, then it hit me just as my hearing began to return, he was yelling, "Rod! Rod, are you hit? Are you okay, Rod?"

He called me by my nickname; if he had called me Rodriguez, I would have known that I looked worse than I felt.

"I'm good!" I shouted over the ringing in my ears, assuming that everyone's ears would be equally damaged, "Keep us moving!"

Mission after mission, deployment after deployment, went by just like the endless sand dunes and patches of the road in my patrols. Staying busy–helped to run the time down. If I stayed focused on my tasks, it hardly mattered that people were trying to aim at, shoot, blow up, or otherwise maim us. You did the job, and you let everything else happen. That didn't mean you could space out and neglect your surroundings. You always had to be on alert for anything, and I mean anything.

Death was a constant companion out there in the desert. You respected it. You didn't fear it. If you did, the Grim Reaper would surely move in on you.

Anything other than testosterone and discipline was unacceptable when shit hit the fan. Training dictated every action and experience demanded emotional detachment. Every life we lost was a sharp slap of reality. However, you didn't get to grieve -- not until the job was completed. You kept focused and took care of the business at hand.

Each tour started to drag longer with every lost friend. You carried them with you. That wasn't really a choice, but you could choose to let that weigh you down like a seventy-five-pound rucksack, or you could decide to let them push you to greater heights. I chose the latter. They made me immune to pain; the sight of blood and instinct to survive for their sake motivated me. Kicking ass and killing anyone who threatened my squad became my nature.

Days turned into months without rest. I felt like a robot, in perpetual motion, moving from the war-torn area to another war-torn area. Kill terrorists here, maintain peace there. Trying to remember the events from one week to the next was like watching a silent film with no color and no sound. Everything seemed almost as if detached like it wasn't my life. Then suddenly, there would be bursts of color, and then memories stuck out from the rest.

Metal clinked against metal, which was the sound of the Humvee's engine vibrating through the cockpit. Everything outside was brown, not because of some sepia film effect, but because that was what the damn desert always looked like -- dusty brown.

Someone coughed. The lead vehicle was throwing up dust from the poorly maintained road; that was if you could even call it a road.

"If I die here, hide my porn stash," somebody shouts from the back.

The soldiers who heard him burst into fits of laughter. I smirked, amused by the banter. The thought of death had become trivial for us.

"Don't jinx us, you dumb ass!" the team commander shouted back.

Everyone laughed again. Chuckling, I nudged the driver with my forearm, offering him some sunflower seeds.

Everyone settles down and goes back to staring out at the sand. "Pass me a Rip It."

Having stayed up to an ungodly hour the night before, I badly needed the drink. Each beautiful silver can contained more caffeine than a cup of coffee. Mana for any soldier stuck with night duties or the early morning watch.

BOOM! BOOM! BOOM!

One second, I'm reaching for the energy drink being handed to me, and the next was chaos as three bombs exploded around our vehicle.

Why didn't the lead vehicle set them off? I wondered in a haze as I was jostled between bodies and the hard steel frame. Funny how you can wonder about the most trivial thing when your life is in danger. The sound of yelling seemed distant at first, almost slow motion, and then everything rushed back to real-time as the adrenaline kicked in throughout my body.

My head had hit fiercely against the metal latch of the seatbelt. A light touch to my temple confirmed that I was bleeding, but I was more concerned about the guys in the back and our driver. One blast would have been enough to lift the Humvee's frame off the ground -- no mean feat. Getting hit by three explosions made a complete mess of the occupants inside. Turning to check on the driver, I saw him bent over the steering wheel.

"BACK UP! BACK UP, NOW!" The commander was wincing and clutching his ribs, but that didn't stop him from being loud enough to motivate the dead.

"I can't! The steering wheel collapsed!" He wasn't in any shape but still determined to carry out his task.

Well, either the driver's been conscious this whole time, or that yelling really can motivate the dead, I snarked to myself as the commander barked the orders again.

"Get us out of the fucking kill zone, now!"

The Humvee lurched backward as the driver slammed the vehicle into reverse. Our front passenger tire was completely gone and had been obliterated by the force of the explosions. Military vehicles were built to handle a lot of punishment, though, and we managed to crawl our way back from the smoking craters in the road. There wasn't much we could do about swerving without a steering wheel, but a straight line retreat was better than no retreat at all. I scanned the horizon for hostiles. Were these bombs left behind - a message of destruction meant to cripple us and keep us paranoid, or were they the beginning of another ambush?

When nothing materialized along the dune ridge, we had to take the risk of assuming the former. We needed to stop and assess our damage. The lead vehicle in our convoy had circled around and skidded to a stop in front of us as we began slowly dismounting, weapons at the ready.

"Little help here!" the driver groaned. There hadn't been time to pay attention when we were escaping, but the steering wheel hadn't just collapsed, the driver had collapsed *onto* it as well. Concerned looks flashed across many of the squad's faces. Were we going to have to pull him off the steering column? Big wounds like that were bad news when you were out in the middle of a patrol with only a medic's kit to patch you up.

Seeing the worry on our faces, he laughed. "I'll live," he said with a look that was somehow both amused and strained. "I'm just stuck."

Pulling him out wasn't easy, especially with everyone looking over their shoulders for the ambush that still hadn't materialized. Once he was free, though, everyone allowed themselves to relax a little. Burned, bruised, and bleeding, we definitely looked like we'd just been through the grinder. I guess it's true, whatever doesn't kill you makes for a great story back at base.

***

I reached for the bowl, resting next to my laptop at the dining table. The clink of sunflower seeds falling from between my fingers as I grabbed a handful mixed with the sound of intermittent typing from my free hand. My eyes were beginning to ache from the hours of being knee-deep in browser tabs on legal studies and anything related to my situation that I could find.

Blowing out a breath of exasperation, I sat back and closed my eyes, momentarily. Salt became the focus for my senses as I tongued at a seed stuck between my teeth. Flashes of dirt roads and sandy dunes crept into my imagination -- gloved hand, filled with sunflower seeds, and then explosions. Blood. Screaming...

I shook my head and dispelled the memories. Grabbing at the bowl, I spat the unfinished seeds back in with their unchewed counterparts. Better to waste it; my day was hard enough without letting a snack cause that kind of shit.

The sound of keys rattling in the door brought me back out of my research a few hours later. *Diana must be home,* I thought, glancing at the clock. I'd lost track of time. I could feel the stiffness in my joints as I realized I hadn't moved from my seat since that afternoon.

Spotting me at the table, she kicked off her shoes and made a beeline for me as I stood. The impact of her hug rocked me back onto my heels. The check for my funeral expenses had badly shaken us.

"Tell me everything," she said, her eyebrows furrowed together.

Normally, I'm a reasonably non-expressive person. Diana let me get away with my vague, deflecting attitude most of the time, but she wasn't having it today. We sat back down together on the couch this time, and she proceeded to interrogate me for the next half hour. I resisted the urge to spout my rank and serial number at the barrage of questions. Humor got me through a lot of tough spots in life, but I knew I needed to take this seriously, for my sake, and to keep Diana from getting too stressed on my behalf. By the time dinner rolled around, we had talked through the shock of receiving funeral funds that the mood almost felt normal. As normal as tacos when you're legally dead can be, anyway.

That normality didn't last long. Getting up the next morning felt like a chore. When I finally got tired of staring at the ceiling, I sat up with a quiet grunt. Typically, I'd consider myself an optimistic person, but today was decidedly a "glass-half-empty" kind of day. It felt like an anti-holiday, declared explicitly to torment me -- "Visit to the VA Regional Office in NYC Day."

Showered, shaved, and dressed, I took the stairs instead of my morning run. Out of habit, I decided to check the mail as I exited the building. Another check of dead man's funds stared back at me from the pile as I sifted through the junk.

Great. Just great.

Every new document I received felt like a nail in my coffin and a testament to my death.

Tearing open the envelope across the Department of the Treasury logo, I pulled out the inner paperwork to skim with morbid curiosity. "Holy shit!"

I cursed vehemently, under my breath, as I took in the amount. It wasn't just another $300 trickle payment; it was a lump sum; and a big one. To top it off, the amount was written to be paid to the order of my ex-wife. Now, that was messed up in every way.

Part of me wanted to rip the checkup. It symbolized everything wrong with my situation. Plus, if it somehow got cashed, I could only imagine how much more complicated everything could become. However, the more logical side of me knew I needed to keep in a safe place and never cash it. Every piece of paperwork I received would have to be accounted for if I was going to get this situation investigated and resolved smoothly.

I took the R train to 59th Street and then made my way to an express train in Manhattan. It took me about thirty minutes to get within a couple of blocks to the regional office.

Not bad for the MTA, I thought, my optimism creeping through.

Stress started to replace the short-lived positivity as I weaved through the foot traffic as I left the station. I couldn't stop thinking about how fucked the whole situation was for me. There wasn't even room for my brain to process all the possible "what if" scenarios. Every development seemed like an unexpected sucker punch and encounterable.

I needed to calm down; and quickly. Whipping out my cell phone, I started to record everything I was thinking including how I felt from day one, the useless phone calls to the V.A., the funeral checks, and everything up to now. My ranting had started to run in circles, but just talking it out loud was cathartic.

"Sir, you cannot shoot inside the premises," a security guard called out as I entered the building.

So much for my little self-therapy. Grabbing a small plastic bin from the screening area, I placed my phone inside along with my wallet and some loose change. "I have an appointment with an attorney... Jim Todd," I told the guard as I stepped through the metal detector.

"Take the escalator to the next floor and make a right," he replied, directing me with a wave of his hand.

Nodding my thanks, I retrieved my various items, stowing them in their appropriate pockets before heading in the indicated direction.

There was nothing maze-like about the building's set up, but I still felt like I was walking through some test. *No... maybe test isn't the right word. Judgment. This place feels judgmental. And cold.* That second one was probably the AC, however.

I stepped through a door and found myself in an office. A line of veterans, waiting to be assisted, snaked away from a desk positioned against the far wall. The limited seating was all occupied. It almost felt like being at the DMV, and everyone who was getting their license had the lingering habits of boot camp instilled in them.

"How may I help you?" The VA rep inquired as I approached the front of the line.

"I was declared dead by the VA, and the attorney on the phone asked me to visit for verification." I talked about my death so casually at this point that I almost forgot this wasn't a normal problem for someone to have.

Equally unphased by my statement, he handed me a sworn statement to complete and gave me a number to wait for my turn. Once I filled out my form, I started scrolling my phone aimlessly. *I should use this time wisely and study*; a nagging thought pestered deep inside of me. My studies were really getting neglected by the constant assault of other priorities.

Procrastination won out in the end, though, as it usually did. Two hours passed, and my phone battery steadily drained by the mobile games and social media I visited as I waited.

After a frustratingly long wait, finally, the sound of the desk clerk calling my number arrived. Stepping through another door behind the reception desk, I found myself in a small office. Windowless and sparsely decorated, the only thing to draw my eye was a wilting plant on the case worker's desk. He gestured for me to sit.

I introduced myself, but I could tell that I was just another number in a long day of names for him. I summarized the details of my case as succinctly as I could. While the earlier assistant hadn't batted an eye at my predicament, this guy looked at me as if I was reading a piece of fiction to him. After repeating my story for the umpteenth time, he asked for almost every identification I had in my wallet to confirm that I was whom I claimed to be. It was both ironic and frustrating that the diligence they were putting into making sure no one claimed my dead identity hadn't been exercised to keep me alive in the first place.

Having taken all of my information, including copies of the letter and both checks, he assured me they would clear everything up. "It will take a few weeks before everything is completely back to normal. You will receive a letter from us confirming your visit," he said, gathering my documents and placing them on a stack of other folders on the corner of his desk.

I thanked him for his time, mentally crossing my fingers that this visit would pan out the way he was promising it would.

Through the door, past the metal detectors, and back outside the building, I took a deep breath of the fresh afternoon air. Well, as fresh as you can get in the middle of Manhattan. Things were looking up. I didn't want to get ahead of myself; I knew that there was still a long road ahead to bury this thing - pun intended. Today's visit felt like a big step in the right direction. Pulling out my phone, I decided to start recording my thoughts once again. The camera was like my personal therapist.

Walking as I talked, I smelled the enticing aroma of grease and hot cheese wafting out of one of the buildings on the street corner. *Why the Hell not*? I thought as I patted down my pockets to make sure I hadn't forgotten my wallet.

I had already skipped my workout today, and maybe pepperoni pizza wasn't one of my approved proteins but being dead was hard work, and I deserved a treat.

I devoured one slice of pizza before I could even find a seat; the cheat meal improved my mood. Deciding to spread the good cheer, I called Diana to give her the good news. "What is it now?" She did not sound as excited as I.

Diana tended to take things with uncertainty and suspicion. It drove me crazy sometimes, but it was part of what made us such a good couple. She balanced out my optimism and flakiness with her reliable stubbornness and her feet firmly grounded in reality.

"Are you sure you're good?" She sounded apprehensive. "Because that agency has a bad reputation for destroying people's lives."

I could visualize the lines furrowing her brow in worry through the phone.

"I know, Babe, but all I can do for now is wait. It's out of my hands. They told me it would be a few weeks, and then everything would be cleared up.

"Fine," she said with a small huff.

"Let's do something fun tonight. Meet me in the city for wings and beer."

I was not going to let future problems overshadow my celebratory mood. We coordinated where we would meet and zeroed in on what time she'd be free. Our favorite spot was a dive, but we didn't mind. There was something about the aesthetic of the rundown seating, the too-loud jukebox, and the faint smell of greasy bar food that just made you forget about the outside world.

I got there first and occupied a small booth in the corner. A bored-looking bartender called out, asking what I wanted without bothering to walk over.

Diana arrived at the same time as the wings and greeted me with a short wave and a smile.

Any long-form discussion would have to wait until our mouths were free as we both started tearing into the plate in front of us. That was fine. We had all night to talk, and I knew we'd have no trouble coming up with topics just like I knew we didn't have any problems with comfortably doing our own thing around each other without feeling the awkward urge to fill the silence.

The night cruised along. One beer turned into two; then three. We then took off for an evening walk through one of the nicer parts of the city. We stopped by a 7-Eleven for snacks and Slurpees. Diana wrapped her arm around mine, we joked and laughed and teased each other about nonsensical things. It felt like it used to, and it felt like I was alive. Now, I just needed the VA to get the memo.

By the time we arrived home, the rest of the neighborhood had already gone to sleep. I quietly rustled through my pockets for the keys. They jingled lightly in my hand. I chuckled as Diana quickly walked past me, barely taking the time to kick off her shoes before falling face-first onto the bed. "Mmm, the bed is soft, it feels good," she mumbled into the mattress.

I smiled as I took my time preparing to join her. By the time I'd slipped under the covers, she was already breathing deeply, her face relaxed in sleep.

I had wanted to tell her I was going to see a doctor tomorrow, but I didn't want to ruin the mood. She was already taking on so much stress with my situation, that adding more didn't feel right. It was probably nothing, anyway -- a small lump on my chest that I'd noticed in the shower and seemed like it wasn't a big deal.

I wanted the doctor to tell me those words out loud, "That it was nothing."

The next morning, Diana left for work bright and early. She usually didn't bother waking me whenever our schedules didn't line up; we liked to let the other person relax and do their own thing. It was a nice change of pace from the military. Unfortunately, I had my plans today. As the door clicked shut, I heard her lock the deadbolt from the outside, and I pulled myself out of bed for my appointment.

The VA clinic felt like your typical government-funded facility -- clean-ish, but not polished, brightly lit, but not welcoming and always busy and crowded. When the doctor finally called me into the examination room, I gave her a brief rundown of my problem.

"Can you take your shirt off please so I can see what you are talking about?" she asked.

"Sure," I replied.

She placed her hand on my chest, pushing and prodding with her fingertips. There it was. She felt around the lump for its boundaries. Behind her trained, unemotional exterior, I wondered what she was thinking. *How long did you say you had this for again?* I imagined her asking. *Why? If I admit that I ignored it at first, hoping it would go away, does that mean it's too late?*

"When did you first notice the lump?" she asked, giving my worries a voice.

"I'm not sure, maybe a few weeks ago. But it just recently started hurting," I murmured, still trying to avoid mentally confronting this as an actual problem.

"All right. Well, just to be safe, I'm going to send you for a mammogram up in the women's clinic on the third floor. Just give them your name and the nurse will assist you right away."

Right away, huh? I thought. Considering the VA's track record of waiting rooms and long lines, I couldn't decide if being given preferential treatment was a blessing or another reason to be worried.

"Good morning, how may I help you?" A nurse greeted me with a smile as I stepped out of the elevator onto the third floor. I gave her my name, and she pulled up my file. "Right this way, please." She brought me to another examining room. "I need you to take off your shirt."

As I pulled off my shirt for the second time, she started setting up some big clamping machine. After fiddling with it for a few moments, she frowned theatrically. "Most of the patients that come through here aren't quite so... bulky," she teased with a smile. "I'm afraid you have way too much muscle on your chest for this."

I chuckled politely at the flattering observation. "So, what now?"

"I will have to call the doctor back and see if we can do an alternate procedure," she informed me. "You can put your shirt back on while you wait."

About twenty minutes later, the doctor from downstairs came and decided that an ultrasound would be an appropriate substitute. The procedure took less time than the waiting had. Quick and painless. Once it was finished, it was time to sit down with the doctor in her office.

Then came the "C" word I was afraid of hearing. She asked if I had a history of cancer in my family. I was happy to say "No" to that one -- at least as far as I was aware.

"It may just be a cyst on your chest," she said. "So, for now, I will prescribe you some antibiotics, and I will see you next week for an additional exam."

"Should I be worried?" I wanted some reassurance.

"Let's just focus on the antibiotic for now and see where things go in a week," she responded in the straightforward tone typical of doctors.

She's probably great at poker, I joked to myself to try, and distract myself from my worries.

On the way back home, I called a few family members and asked about any health problems. I was right; there was no history of cancer on either side. Finished with my calls, I still had the rest of the day in front of me. Remembering that I'd skipped my workout the day before, I decided a little extra walking wouldn't hurt. I took the long way home, cutting through a park and stopping to feed some ducks along the way. A hotdog stand caught my eye as I continued toward my home, and I convinced myself that I deserved another cheat day after how stressful the week had been.

Slathering my purchase with relish, onions, ketchup - all in enough quantities that walking and eating became a balancing act. I decided it was finally time to stop putting off going home. It wasn't like I wanted to avoid Diana. There wasn't anything I could think of that would make me feel like that, but I'd always been self-sufficient, and I knew how much of a toll my problems took on her. On the other hand, I could already hear her chiding me, lovingly, of course, on how I didn't need to do everything on my own.

I got home and sat down on the sofa to read the instructions on the medicine bottle. Diana came home not long after I got back, and I made the bottle do a vanishing act. She started rambling about how much she hated the traffic and all the construction going on. *I'd rather pay attention to her problems than bring up mine*, I thought, as I made a show of listening intently.

"What do you want to do for dinner?" I asked as she winded down her monologue on the ever-present problems of living in New York City.

"Let's do sushi," she replied, her face brightening. Thinking about food always seemed to lighten her mood.

"Sounds good to me," I said. "You want a drink? I need a drink."

"You okay?" she asked.

Whoops. "Yeah, I'm fine. It's just been a long day."

"Okay, well…" She shrugged. "It must be a happy hour somewhere."

There was a pretty decent Japanese place down the street. At first, I debated taking the time and effort to go out again versus getting delivery, but my desire to put back some sake shots won over in the end.

The sun had set at some point while I had been inside. Wrapping her arm in mine, Diana made a pointed effort to try to catch my gaze. "Are you sure you're okay?" she asked.

"I'm fine," I replied. I tried to make the reply seem casual. Her furrowed brow told me that I'd failed.

"All right…" she said.

Her tone invited me, practically begged me, to open up, but I just smiled and squeezed her arm. Why ruin a good night of food and drinks with more problems? "It's just stress. Being dead is less relaxing than I've been led to believe."

Maybe if I gave her a convincing argument, she'd stop reading into what was bothering me. Besides, it wasn't entirely untrue. I'm sure my mood was probably at least partially due to the constant weight of dealing with the VA. The doctor said the lump might be a cyst, anyway. That's not nearly as stressful as wading through bureaucracy. I kept telling myself that, but I don't think my subconscious was any more convinced than Diana.

Dinner flew by. I was too preoccupied with my thoughts to pay much attention to what I ate, and I'm sure I wasn't very good company. The drinks didn't do much to calm my brain, either; not in the quantities, I was letting myself drink, anyway. Ordering too many shots would only make Diana even more suspicious.

"Can you just get out of your head and hold me tonight?" she said, jostling me as we climbed into bed.

I accepted my duties and held her close like the good boyfriend I was.

Pulling myself out of bed at dawn was harder than I would have liked. So many cheat days recently had me afraid that I'd fall off the wagon and stop working out entirely. *No way I'll let my problems take that from me too*, I thought.

Shoes laced, I shut the door quietly behind me and went for a run. When I got back, Diana was getting ready to leave for work.

"You're up early," she commented, downing her juice in one long gulp.

"Yeah, I just wanted to get a quick run in before I started my day."

A noise of acknowledgment, a peck on the cheek, and she was out the door. As soon as she left, I was back online, but instead of looking up VA horror stories, I was intent on finding out more about the thing growing inside of me. Then again, according to the internet, a stubbed toe was a symptom of cancer, flesh-eating disease, and a million other things. *Maybe I should stick to the VA horror stories.* Glancing toward the bedroom, I remembered the pill bottle stashed under the spare blanket in the closet.

The bottle said, "With or without food," but I always hated the queasiness of dealing with meds on an empty stomach. Blending myself a post-run protein shake, I started idly reading the rest of the label on the bottle while I waited. I was mid-mouthful of my first gulp when my phone buzzed. It was the VA clinic asking me to come in for a blood test. I set an appointment for a couple of hours later. No point in waiting around, hoping the pills worked when I could narrow it down today. Before she hung up, the doctor asked again if my family had a history of cancer. I really didn't like that question.

"No, I double-checked," I said firmly.

I showered, changed my clothes, and started making my way to the clinic. I didn't have a good excuse if Diana came home and saw that I wasn't there, so I just crossed my fingers that she wouldn't get off work early.

After giving the tech my information, she took me to the lab. Over the next half an hour, it felt like they'd taken half a liter of blood. Honestly, it must have been at least eight vials. Enough to make a vampire jealous.

Back in the office, the doctor smiled and gestured for me to take a seat. "I would like to do a biopsy on the lump sometime next week if the medication doesn't appear to be effective. Is that okay?"

"I'll get back to you on that. I have to figure out my work schedule." My schedule was fine; I simply didn't know how I was going to break the news to Diana. It was important to me that I not worry her, but I didn't like keeping things from her, and the longer this went on, the more excuses I'd have to make up for these appointments.

"All right, Mr. Rodriguez. Well, let's set you up with a temporary appointment date, and if it doesn't work out, you can call and reschedule. That way we don't end up in a situation where you're free and we don't have any time to see you. Sound good?"

I assented, and we hashed out the details for when I'd most likely be free. Paperwork satisfied, she handed me a slip to give to one of the other staff members on the way out. One last stop at the front desk, and I was back out under the morning sun. I blinked a few times, adjusting to the difference between the clinic's harsh fluorescent lights and the bright yellow daylight outside. Checking my phone, I noticed one missed call. Diana. My phone must have lost its signal inside the building. Pressing the voicemail button, I stood and shaded my vision with one hand while listening to the message with the other.

"I don't know what's going on," the voicemail said, "but you usually pick up, and lately you've been acting distant. Are you mad at me? Please call me back."

I'd already resolved to tell her what was going on, but I was going to put it off until dinner, at least. Something like this deserved a face-to-face conversation. At least that had been my excuse to put it off for a little while longer. Now I felt like I needed to call her back immediately. I took a deep breath and pressed the speed dial for her cell. She picked up quickly but didn't berate me for the way I'd been behaving. She was never the type of person to attack me for anything. I am always understanding, always ready to be there even when I wouldn't accept the help. Instead, she let me ease into it. We small-talked a bit.

She said she was not going to school tonight because she wanted to go to a basketball game at the Barclay Center. Eventually, the reason I'd called seemed to be too far off track for how easygoing the conversation had become. This happened a lot with us. We would be on the verge of a meaningful conversation and just get distracted talking about whatever small things were on our minds.

We made plans for dinner and hung up the phone. *Damnit.* I'd gotten the reprieve I'd decided I didn't want. I would have to tell her first thing that evening.

Diana came home to the sound of me throwing up in the bathroom.

She banged on the door.

"Are you okay?" she shouted.

"Yes, just give me a minute." My insides felt like they wanted to jump out of my throat, but I tried to keep my voice steady. I flushed the toilet, brushed my teeth and splashed my face with water. My reflection in the mirror was less than motivating, but I could tell Diana was hovering by the door, waiting for an update.

She gave me a look of mixed concern and indignation.

"What's going on with you?"

I told her I was fine. Why did I hold back? Maybe I felt cornered.

"No, you're not! I know something is going on, and you're just not telling me!" Diana puts up with a lot of my shit, but I could tell she was at the end of her rope.

"I'm fine, why don't you just get off my back?" This wasn't how I'd planned the evening going. I wanted to tell her, but something inside me kept pushing back. Confronted with any hostility, my first reaction was to be equally hostile, not to curl up and surrender.

Even as I pushed past her to storm off toward the bedroom, I could hear the concern in her voice. "Babe, I'm worried about you. What's going on?" She was trying to get through to me as she did everything she could to keep her temper in check, and mine.

I sat on the edge of the bed, refusing to make eye contact but not leaving when she sat by my side in turn.

"Please, just talk to me," she said, wrapping me in her arms.

Finally, I found the words, or the words found me. I told Diana everything. From the moment I'd discovered the unwelcomed lump on my chest, to my appointments over the past couple of days, and my present state of mystery diagnosis. I walked to the closet and pulled out my hidden stash to show her the paperwork and meds I had gotten from the doctor.

"Why do you insist on doing things like this alone?" she said, prodding me in the ribs with one finger. She wasn't mad, and she didn't hate me for hiding it. She was chiding me, sure, but in the loving, caring way that told me she cared. Suddenly I felt like a huge idiot for keeping it from her in the first place.

"Just do me a favor," I said. "Don't tell anyone about this until I get a better idea of what this is. The last thing I need is for my phone to be blowing up because I have a nosy family."

"Deal, but I still get to be nosy," she replied before standing. "Now I'm going to go take a shower and wash all this work grime off. Do you need anything, first?"

I shook my head, no.

Nodding, she grabbed a towel and disappeared into the bathroom. As the sound of running water filled the apartment, I breathed a sigh of relief. Keeping my health issues hidden from Diana had been slowly gutting me. That night I finally slept with a clear conscience.

CHAPTER 4

It's true that war and violence can fundamentally change a person. Sometimes in movies, they'll say that you get desensitized to it and that the first time was hard, but eventually, it's just part of the job. That wasn't true for me. Snipers capable of ending lives unexpectedly between one breath and the next, explosions indiscriminately taking limbs and friends took their last breaths in my arms all took its tax on my soul, one piece at a time. In the moment, maybe, I felt strong. A hero with a gun and a purpose, but underneath, I was suffering all the same affected by trauma without even realizing it.

Sometime during my third year of deployment, we were called on a mission into the farming area along the triangle of death in Baghdad, Iraq. We had no idea what we were getting ourselves into in this worn-torn country.

"Grab some extra ammo, Rod," My platoon leader commanded as he started lining his vest with extra magazines and a spare grenade or two. We all knew any work in or near the triangle of death required we pack heavy.

The team was almost ready to go, minus one. The driver of my truck was missing. We were scheduled to leave in the next two minutes, and I didn't want to be part of the vehicle causing delays. I scanned the camp from my position in the turret. Suddenly, the driver emerged from behind a nearby tent, panting and carrying a full case of what looked like ice-cold Rip-Its. I could hear Sarge cussing up a storm somewhere in the distance, and I suddenly knew what was happening.

"We got to go, now!" yelled the driver as he came skidding to a stop next to the truck. "Help me load these up and let's go!"

"What the fuck did you do?" I said incredulously. I wasn't exactly mad at being able to take all those cold cans out into the hot ass desert, but I didn't need to be chewed out by the sarge either.

"You do know I will fuck you up when you get back, right?" *Speak of the devil.* "Since you need those cans so bad, I will put some water on my knee so that when I kick your ass, you can quench that thirst," he added.

"Roger that, Sarge. Looking forward to it, Sarge," the driver replied smartly as he quickly climbed up behind the steering wheel. He knew he would get away with it; no way, Sarge held up the convoy over a little discipline but the driver was toeing a fine-line of disrespect for when he eventually got back to camp.

"Oh, so you think you're a smart ass? We'll see if those drinks were worth it when you get back. Now, eyes up! Do not deny me the pleasure of killing you myself, soldier! Roll out!" he shouted–menacingly before storming off to find someone else to chew out.

"That was close," the driver laughed as the truck's engine rumbled to life. "You're welcome, by the way."

"Thanks for what? We're probably going to go down with you for that little stunt. If you're going to sneak drinks, at least have a little discretion!" I replied, lightly kicking him from my spot in the gunner's harness.

"Hey, watch it!" I felt him swat my leg. "I'll take the dive when we get back, okay? Just quit kicking me, or I'm going to end up swerving us into a ditch."

Everyone chuckled and settled into a watchful silence.

It was perfect weather, a slight breeze to counter a warm September. It reminded me of home and was perfect for a motorcycle ride; no destination, just the sun on your back and wind on your face.

The truck skidded to a halt, jerking me out of my thoughts. We had arrived in a small village, but it looked like a ghost town. There was no foot traffic, and even the usual stray animals, were absent. On the one hand, most ambushes tried hard not to be this obvious. On the other, you took nothing for granted out here in the desert.

"Gunners, heads on a swivel; this could be a setup," my mic crackled as the team leader started issuing orders.

"Contact, at one o'clock," I said through the comms.

This village was technically under our protection, making any village classified as a friendly assuming he was whom he appeared to be.

"Help me, Mista; please help me." The man's face was streaked with tears as he approached, trying to communicate with us in less than perfect English.

Several squad dismounted, scanning the area while the team leader talked to him in Arabic. It was an essential part of our training to gain a basic understanding of the local language, but I could only catch maybe half of what he was saying.

"They took my family," he cried.

Any village that openly accepted help from the US forces was a soft target for this kind of retaliation. All the poor man wanted was peace for his people, but according to the snatches of conversation, I could follow, last evening terrorists had invaded his home, beat him bloody and taken his family as hostage.

As we gathered the information on his family, we began to etch out a few locations based on local intel and our satellites. We had barely left the outskirts of the village and started to drive past a farm when one of the locals flagged us down. It turned out the man had witnessed the whole thing, including a family being dragged off and screams of distress near a ridgeline farther down the road.

When we started to near the location, we could see a plume of black smoke rising from somewhere beyond our line of sight. An abandoned house, charred to its framework, stood in the middle of another expanse of farmland. This kind of destruction served a double purpose sending a threatening message to anyone that cooperated with the US military and also erased any evidence that we could use to help track the terrorists later.

We pulled up to the burned remains and began unloading. Every truck formed its group as we swept around opposite sides of the building and out into the field. Guns up, we swiftly covered the open ground and began surrounding the property. Silently gesturing, the team commander pointed at the outline of a ditch that had been dug on the far side of the house.

"Eyes on the ditch," he whispered on the mic as we all nodded.

Guns pointed, we moved on our stomachs and elbows to avoid visibility as we approached the ditch. I can still remember every detail of that horrific sight. A wave of sharp inhales and clenched teeth swept over the squad as our eyes darted down into the ditch.

A small lake of blood and twelve dead bodies stared back up at us. The smell was overwhelming, but it didn't drive everyone away before the image had burned into our memories.

Three adults and nine kids. Nine.

The brutes had slaughtered them like animals. A member of one of the other squads started throwing up while the rest of us clenched our jaws and fought not to puke or pass out. Suddenly, a woman screamed from somewhere behind me.

Abdullah Ameeri had arrived with the rest of the villagers; he'd either tailed us or seen the smoke column on his own and decided to investigate. Everything turned to screams and howling as the villagers took in the sight. After a while, everyone started moving to pick up each body from the ditch.

On the surface, I felt numb, but somewhere in my head, I could feel every scream and cry screeching away at my heart. *Need to stay alert in case of an ambush,* I told myself, forcing my attention on anything that wasn't the carnage around me.

All these civvies were milling around, soldiers staring at the ground and the sky, and their gazes gave off a thousand-yard stare. This would be a perfect opportunity for a follow-up strike.

I kept repeating that logic to myself, and it helped to take my mind off of what was right in front of me. Once we had collected all the bodies, our mission objective changed. Our new orders were to escort the villagers through Baghdad, making sure that they reach the funeral home safely.

As our convoy started making its way toward the highway, one of the villager's pick-up trucks blew a tire. It fishtailed to a stop and the bodies in the back of the vehicle tumbled out all over the highway, bringing back what was proving to be a stubborn nightmare. Considering the effect that the sight had on me, I can't imagine what it did to the villagers who knew and loved the deceased.

The area where their truck broke down was a major kill zone. As soon as we stopped, all traffic on the highway halted. Sitting still like that was a terrible feeling. Everyone was hyper-alert, scrambling to redistribute the bodies among the other vehicles. We didn't have time to fix the tire even given our attempt at haste, and we were still sitting ducks when we started taking sniper fire.

Even though we were expecting it or something like it, we had no clue where the fire had originated. From my machine gun position, I could see the body of one of the dead children still splayed out in the road. It was a little girl, her pajamas now soaked in her blood. She was maybe four or five years old. I was scanning the horizon for the sniper but the body of the girl kept drawing my gaze until one of the villagers grabbed her limp body off the ground and started running toward my truck.

"Mista, Mista, please! Please help!" he cried out. He extended his arms forward, presenting her body like he was offering a sword.

Fighting my instinct to cry, I pulled the girl's body from his offering hands. Suddenly her long hair fell from her face revealing nothing but a large exit wound from a bullet passing through her forehead.

My world slowed down as my memory captured that moment forever. The scent of blood in the air, the wind slightly blowing on my face, the taste of sweat on my lips, her beautiful face marred with that wound, and the horror frozen in her expression were now engraved in my memory.

What is this? Why am I here? I kept repeating.

I felt a powerful left hook from my team leader, hitting my thighs inside the Humvee's cabin.

"Get on that gun! Get on that gun!" He yelled. "Hot Rod, get on that fucking gun!"

I snapped out of my daze. Two minutes is an eternity on the battlefield, and I'd been in my little world while my squad was in danger. Someone had figured out the general direction the fire was coming from, but they didn't have the firepower to do anything but take pot shots of their own. Following their lead, I started to light up the hill they'd been aiming toward.

This gave us enough of a window to finish loading the bodies onto other trucks. Wheels skidded on hot pavement and the convoy shot off, putting enough distance between the sniper that we were officially out of danger for now. The rest of the drive was, thankfully, was uneventful.

We got the villagers to the funeral home and stood guard until dusk. Nobody said anything on the way back. That moment scarred us all. I knew that little girl was going to stay with me for a very long time.

The camp was busy with normal day-to-day activities when we got back -- soldiers moved the supplies, walked patrol, and shot the shit as if nothing had happened. I guess, technically, nothing had occurred for anyone that wasn't in our convoy. Not that these guys didn't have their fubar missions and mental scars of their own.

For the rest of the evening, we were on standby. My driver and I headed over to the platoon sergeant's trailer to receive our due punishment. The antics of this afternoon seemed like they'd happened years ago.

I knocked on the door and waited. He didn't say much as we entered, just looked at the both of us as he set down a clipboard he'd been writing on. "You guys good?" he asked.

"Yeah, Sarge," we responded in tandem. I'm sure we both wanted to say otherwise, but soldiers are rarely the expressive type.

"Check on the other guys, see how they're doing, then report back to me."

"Yes, Sarge." As we went around, we found that all the men were as tightlipped with us as we had been with the sergeant. Whatever turmoil they had swimming in their heads, they would deal with it alone, in their own way. That was the life of soldiers.

"Everyone is good, Sarge," I said as we entered his trailer.

He raised an eyebrow in a way that said I doubt that, but instead, he just said, "Copy that. Now get out of here."

"Yes, Sarge, copy that," we responded. It wasn't often that a planned punishment was diminished.

We split up after leaving the sergeant's tent. I went to my trailer, threw my vest over my face, and tried to get some shut-eye. No matter how tired I was, though, the little girl and her wound kept appearing in front of my eyes. *It's going to be a sleepless night.*

Still, I kept my eyes tightly shut, like every other soldier in the camp.

***

She stood against me, her silk black hair dancing slowly across her face. Even though I couldn't see her properly, I could tell she was beautiful, with soft baby skin. We were outside, and the light shone brightly on her outstretched arms and pale blue pajamas; I heard her giggle as she rotated in place, soaking up the warmth of the sun.

"Hey, who are you?" I grabbed her attention. She turned toward me as a gust of wind blew across her face. Blood oozed from the hole where her forehead and the right eye were supposed to be. She looked at me with her remaining eye filled with immense sadness.

My heart lurched at the sight. It was no longer bright and sunny. My nostrils flared as they filled with the stench of blood and smoke. My eyes fixated on her fatal injuries. I reached out reflexively as she suddenly slumped hard on the ground. I screamed at her to wake up.

"I wanted to help you. I am so sorry." My voice was hoarse and heavy, laden with tears. "I wanted to…"

***

"Wake up," she said. "Babe, wake up."

No, it wasn't the dead girl speaking to me. Diana's voice called out again, pulling me from the shackles of the nightmare. Dripping with sweat, I sat up in bed, back in my apartment. Cold November air seeped in through the window and chilled against my skin. I looked over toward her, panting, short of breath. For a moment, I stared at her like she was a stranger.

"It was a nightmare, Babe," Diana said, her grip on my arm relaxing now that she'd shaken me awake.

I shivered, both from the cold air and the strange vibes of the nightmare still creeping along my body. I ran my hands across my face and over my head while blowing out an exasperated breath.

"Sorry," I said numbly. I had been dealing with nightmares since the days of my service, and they had become a recurring theme of my life. I groaned.

Recurring themes aside, life continued to slog along. My schoolwork had been suffering recently, a casualty of my continually shifting priorities. I barely managed to make it through my midterms and had to promise myself that I'd put more effort into the finals. They'd selected me in an MBA program majoring in International Economy after I cleared my undergrad degree at Berkeley College. It was my future and having it suddenly become secondary was crushing.

Diana and I were swamped with work and studies. We had a quiet Thanksgiving dinner at home and visited our close family when we had a chance. Things had been getting better; well, except the weather. It had been colder than usual that month. November came and went, and I kept waiting for the promised confirmation letter from the VA.

It was a foggy morning in early December when it finally arrived. I was getting ready for a morning jog and opened the door to see the mailman getting ready to knock. Normally, mail would be delivered to our box downstairs, but the government stamp probably prompted him to bring this one to us special delivery -- a letter from the Department of Veteran's Affairs.

Giddy with excitement that this ordeal was finally going to be put to rest, I quickly signed and closed the door behind me with a heartfelt thanks. It would finally end. I ripped the letter open with ecstatic energy buzzing through me.

"This letter is to inform you that due to the death of Carmelo Rodriguez, at the end of this month, all the benefits from this veteran will be cut. We sympathize for your loss. Please contact us if you need further information."

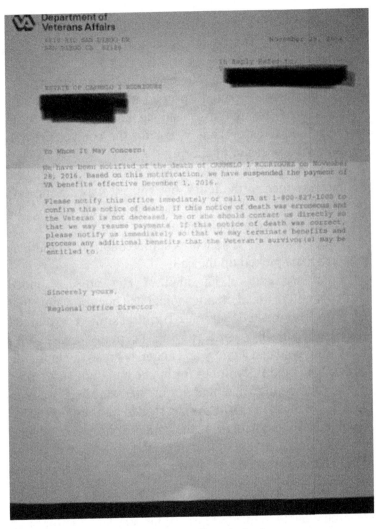

Letter declaring Carmelo dead.

My shoulders sagged as disappointment flooded through my body.

"What the Hell?" I read the letter again and again as the knot in the pit of my stomach tightened.

What did I just read?

I read it twice, again. There was nothing between the lines -- no secret "gotcha!" printed on the back. Diana's words echoed through my head again about how these people ruined lives every day. Par for the course; not that that made it any easier to accept.

All I could logically do at this point was to call the number provided in the letter, but since it was a Saturday, the office was closed. With that phone call out of the question, I decided to make another.

"Babe, it's back." The words spilled out of my mouth as soon as Diana picked up the call.

"What are you talking about?" Her voice sounded startled, and I realized, in my panic, I had been so vague that I'd probably freaked her out. Backtracking, I explained what I meant. It wasn't easy to keep my voice from fluctuating between anxiety and anger as I read the letter out loud to her. I didn't fault her for it; she had done just that.

She seemed to realize that despite her warnings, we both knew this wasn't my fault. As she started rambling on about the mishandling by the VA, the sound of her voice helped me calm down. Even full of fury and spitfire, something about Diana's presence, even over the phone, always helped me focus. *Assess the situation.*

I was back to square one. So, what next? I decided to research what the other veterans did in similar situations and go from there. "Get in touch with you congressman," one article said. Another advised for me to approach a lawyer and reach out to veteran advocates programs.

"Babe, I'll call you back. I'm going to see if I can get a handle on this a different way," I said, the phone still cradled against my shoulder as I'd typed. I could hear a sharp inhale that would inevitably be followed by complaints that I was trying to do everything alone again, so I added, "I'll fill you in once you get home from work."

This seemed to appease Diana enough that she hung up with only a small grumble that I'd interrupted her rant about how shitty the system was. I grinned. Only that woman could make me want to smile while I was dealing with a situation like this. I spent the rest of the afternoon reaching out to about twenty lawyers and a few veteran advocates. The results of my efforts were not very encouraging. Nearly half of the time, the calls went to voicemail, and those who were available had no experience with my situation. Not one of them knew how to help. They couldn't even recommend someone who could offer any help. Even though this was an epidemic problem, according to the internet, it felt like every professional I talked to had never heard of it before.

My whole weekend went by seething over how the VA was not only screwing me over but also had done it in a way that almost felt intentional. How else could something so seemingly simple be so hard to fix?

My habit of procrastinating was officially benched. Putting anything off at this point was likely to endanger more than I was willing to risk. So the first thing I did Monday morning was to call the number given in the letter. It took me about an hour to get in touch with an actual person who could help. My complaint almost seemed to leave her speechless at first. Every single one of these calls involved the same reaction -- first, the confused silence. Then a barrage of questions as the person on the other end of the phone tried to wrap their head around the problem. She asked me to explain things to her in more detail so that she could make a note of it for her documents. I wondered what was the point of a briefing when I had given them the details a dozen times to start from the beginning every time.

She put me on a brief hold. After a short wait, she returned with more of the same useless advice. "Sir, file a sworn statement at the regional office," she said. Her professional tone irked me.

"I already did that," I retorted, trying not to let my frustration sour the call and prevent me from getting the help I needed.

"Then, sir, inquire about the regional office if your sworn statement went through or not?"

This was absolute madness. Never in my life had I experienced such a mockery of red tape and circular logic. As a veteran who had dedicated his life to his country, it defied common decency that there was not a single person who could help me in this situation. Out of ideas, I decided to call the regional office and do as the woman said. After yet another circus of transfers, robot voiced menus, and hold music, I was transferred to a case manager only to be told the sworn statement would take more time to process and in the meantime, they could do nothing about it.

***

"There's something wrong with your paperwork, Sir." The staff member behind the desk at the VA clinic said, looking at me dubiously over her monitor. Whatever error was popping up on her screen was enough to put a hold on my medication and enough to get me a stink-eye like I was some criminal, to boot.

"Are you being serious right now?" My temper flared. Even if I wanted to acknowledge that she wasn't directly responsible for whatever was happening, I was sick of running into problems in every aspect of my life.

"I'm sorry, sir, but we will have to mail you the medication once this problem has cleared up." Her face was poker straight.

I pinched the bridge of my nose and ran a hand across the top of my head as if I could wipe the frustration away. "Okay, then can you at least make sure my address is correct, so it is sent to the right location?" Knowing the VA, I was ready to start assuming that anything that could go wrong, would go wrong.

"Sure." She tapped at her keyboard and read the address aloud for me. I could not hold in my incredulous laughter at this point.

Wow. Just wow.

Someone must be intentionally trying to ruin my life. That or the VA's system was so fubar that it would be easier to wipe it clean and start over than to try to sort out the tangled mess it had become. "That is the address of my prior residence. I know I already provided you guys with the updated one." I was at my breaking point.

She ignored my outburst, wordlessly handing me a form to update my address again. Scrawling furiously, I handed it back to her after a quick double-check to make sure that I'd filled it out correctly.

"If you don't receive your medication on time, just go to the emergency room and get a supply from them," she said.

That's the first piece of useful advice I've gotten out of a VA employee in weeks, I thought bitterly.

I walked out of the clinic, practically pulling my hair out, then immediately took out my phone to make an appointment to meet with my doctor. Maybe she'd be more willing to divulge what kind of wrench my file had thrown in the clinic's system or give me a refill on my meds, at the very least. All of my problems were starting to overlap in ways that made everything more complicated.

Diana was right. I needed a lawyer as soon as possible.

A few days later, I sat in the waiting room of the emergency room. My meds had, surprise, surprise, never reached me.

Waiting for hours and hours to get the pettiest issues solved was becoming a norm for me. I pondered over my predicament and how it was affecting me mentally and physically. I was ready to give up just about anything to get it fixed, but then I thought about all the things that the problem was making me give up, and I revised my list not to include those. Once I was called into the examination room, I told the nurse who was assisting me that I needed a refill on my meds. Within the next twenty minutes, I walked out of the hospital with a thirty-day supply. *Now if only everything else could be solved that easily.*

***

"All right, let's do this." My fake enthusiasm was lost on the nurse assisting in my biopsy. A stony blank expression stared back at me as he listed off my chart for the doctor standing next to him.

Before the procedure, she wanted to assess if there was any change in the lump.

"I haven't seen any," I replied when she asked me whether there had been any noticeable differences since my first visit.

She pressed lightly on the lump, causing me to wince. "Did you follow the schedule for the medications?" she asked.

I nodded.

"Then we will go ahead with biopsy once we run an ultrasound."

I sat shirtless on the high bed in the sterile operating room.

She injected local anesthesia to numb the area around my chest; I lost sensation gradually and the numb area grew in time with my heartbeat. *There was nothing to panic about,* I told myself. A little biopsy is kid stuff compared to getting shot at.

The doctor loomed over me, picking at the lump with a long needle and syringe. As I stared at the ceiling, something snapped in me and I felt as if I was transported back to Iraq. Suddenly, I was in the ditch on that farm in Iraq, surrounded by a mass of dead bodies. "You're dead" flashed in front of my eyes and then I snapped back to reality.

"Your procedure is completed, Mr. Rodriguez. We've extracted enough of a sample for testing."

After more paperwork, I was ready to leave. There wasn't any consultation in the doctor's office, and no mention of the C-word this time, thankfully.

Worn out, I took an Uber home instead of walking. My phone rang; it was Diana.

"Why are you not at work?" she asked. She must have called my workplace when I didn't pick up my cell during the procedure.

I told her I had an appointment today with the doctor.

"And?" she asked.

"And what?"

"Stop playing games with me," she commanded.

I told her about the biopsy.

"How are you getting home?"

When I told her about the Uber, she just sighed over the phone.

"I could have been there," she said.

"It was no big deal. I was in and out."

"Okay, I'll be home soon." She'd given in a little quicker than I'd anticipated. I chalked it up to her wisely picking her battles.

I got home and did some homework. I wasn't really in the mood to cook, so I just ate a bowl of cereal. My chest throbbed with pain. I gulped the pain meds and fell asleep.

My eyes crusted over with evidence of my impromptu nap, and I woke to the sound of Diana coming in the front door.

"Let me see you," she said, dropping her purse and coat on the floor as she walked toward me, her lips pursed together and eyes concerned.

I took off the bandage and showed her. Even though the injection was small, my chest muscle had swelled up and was surrounded by a bluish-purple bruise.

"You're so stubborn." She walked out of the room and grabbed the ice pack from the freezer. "Put this on for the swelling.

I followed her orders dutifully as a good soldier and boyfriend should.

The swelling took a week to subside, and the bruise a little longer than that. My chest was finally starting to look normal again just in time for the follow-up appointment with the doctor.

The wait time was its usual pain in the ass, but once I got pulled into her office things went by quickly. As far as visits to the doc went, this one ranked at the top of the list. I stepped out of the clinic with a small bounce in my step. Taking the initiative for once, I called Diana.

"What is it? What did the doctor say?" She did not even let me get out a hello before she started bombarding me with questions.

My heart soared at her concerned voice, I would be stressing out about worrying her, but today I was just touched. My good mood wouldn't let me interpret the situation pessimistically.

"Spit it out, will you, Babe?" her impatient voice brought me back from my thoughts.

"It's nothing! Doc says it's just a benign tumor." I announced, chuckling at her impatience.

"What the fuck is that?"

I could tell she couldn't decide whether to be concerned over my use of the word "tumor" or happy over my apparent nonchalance and use of the word "benign."

"That means it ain't cancerous, and proper medication will make it go away," I explained as she drew a sigh of relief.

"Thank God. All right! That settles it. Let's celebrate tonight." The spark in her voice was back, and that made me even happier than the touching concern from before.

"Let's do it. I'm up for whatever right now."

We ended up dancing the night away at an R&B concert. The next two weeks were as close to bliss as my life was capable of being. My health was sorted, and I engrossed myself in studies and work. All that was left was to keep hoping for the confirmation letter for my sworn statement to come in soon.

***

Since the biopsy and positive response to the medication, my life was heading in a clear direction. That should have been the first warning sign that I was getting complacent. I stared at the caller ID, wondering if this call and the letters from the VA were a punishment. It was my ex-wife, not precisely a knife in the back like being declared dead by the government, but a sucker punch to my recent optimism all the same.

"My dad just received a letter from the Department of Education. They're offering their condolences for our loss. Apparently, you're dead. What is going on?" My ex-wife managed to make the question sound accusatory, as always.

"What?" Even though I'd heard her just fine, the sudden realization that my unique predicament was spreading into this part of my life and past caught me temporarily off guard.

"You better not be trying to scam the government. I will turn you in. I don't want my family involved in this mess. Please tell them to leave us alone," she continued without waiting to hear my defense.

The difference between my ex-wife and Diana was clear as day. One immediately jumped to conclusions and thought the worst of me, while the other stood by me like a rock when I needed support. Some relationships work, others don't. I'd hoped that replacing the latter with the former would have freed me from these kinds of interactions. Apparently the trauma of my deployments wasn't the only part of my past I was having trouble shaking off.

"Send me the letter. I want to see what you have." I kept myself calm and collected despite her petty accusations.

She refused, complaining again that she didn't want to be involved, and making a fuss over the cost of postage to forward it to me. We finally reached a compromise when I told her just to take a picture of the letter.

There it was, offering sympathies. Once the Department of Education received my birth certificate, my student loans would be cleared. "I will contact the authorities regarding this. Thanks," I said, feigning slight ignorance to the cause of this latest mess. No point in trying to explain everything

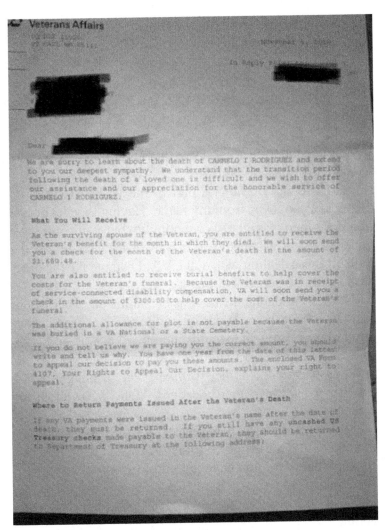

Letter of spousal benefits.

I'd been going through to her. I'd be more likely to be criticized than sympathized with, and I didn't have the patience for that. Instead, I changed the subject. "I will pick up Jaxon over the weekend. Will that be okay?" I always tried to maintain civility between us for the sake of my little boy.

"Fine by me," she retorted before ending the call. No goodbye, and no attempt to hash out a schedule ahead of time to make sure everyone was happy. She hadn't changed one bit.

I immediately called the student aid manager who handled my educational loans.

As I was put on hold, a part of me wished I could let them clear the loans from my name. Having the clean slate of a dead man was, for once, tempting, but you can't have your cake and eat it, too. If I wanted to clear up all the bullshit I was dealing with at the VA, I had to take the debts along with the benefits of being alive.

Navigating phone menus was becoming an expertise for me. Once I got the right person on the phone, I read her the letter and she said she would find out what was going on. She verified my email and the best phone number on file, and that was that. *Another waiting game*, I thought as she asked if I had any other questions. "Oh! What about my financial aid?"

Fingers crossed, I waited while she typed something on the other side of the line. "Still in the financial aid program for this semester. You have nothing to worry about there," she assured me.

Thanking her, I hung up the call. "Nothing to worry about."

I had heard those four words a few times since the problem started. I won't say they were always lying. The people saying them probably believed it. Still, their words stopped comforting me a while back. If push comes to shove, I was ready for the worst-case scenario.

I was about to call Diana, but I couldn't bring myself to press the dial. As much as I wanted her to be involved, I didn't want to pile my stress on her. *At least not until she's off of work*, I convinced myself. So, once again, I said nothing. Once again, I probably should have.

Instead, I decided to try another round of video therapy. Recording my thoughts as they came to mind helped relax my stress. I couldn't afford to let anxiety distract me from my other responsibilities. I had to finish my assignments for the semester. Sitting on a high "C" wasn't the most comfortable place to be.

I sat on my sofa and put on some soft piano music. White noise usually helped me to concentrate. Today, though, I couldn't stop my mind from wandering. Even as I stared down at the laptop, cursor blinking on the blank page, I couldn't help but wonder how my son Jaxon was doing. It had been weeks since I'd seen him. His mother and I were going through a custody battle, which was another ongoing hassle. At least I'd be getting him for the weekend. As soon as Diana got off work, we'd go pick him up together.

A couple of hours passed, and I managed to make some minor progress on my homework before Diana walked in the door. Excited to see my son, I completely forgot that I had told myself I was going to inform her of the letter from the Department of Education. She changed out of her work clothes, and we were back out the door, stopping for groceries at Fort Hamilton base commissary before speeding off to Staten Island to pick up Jaxon on time. His mother despised waiting.

The moment I pulled up, Jaxon saw me and ran toward me with little steps. Spreading my arms, I grabbed him by the armpits and lifted him, twirling him into a big hug. My face was all smiles, but inside it felt bittersweet. I was happy to see him, of course, but I was also sad that I could not be there for him more often. Grabbing his things, I loaded them into the trunk of the car. He had so much he wanted to talk about with me. It was heartwarming to hear him chatter and to watch him get smarter every time we met. I wish I could have been there more.

Over the course of the next forty minutes on the ride home, Jaxon fell asleep. We got back shortly after dark. Between groceries and a sleeping toddler, I figured I could consider the weightlifting portion of my weekly workout fulfilled. The smell of pinecones greeted us as we unlocked the front door. Diana placed a basket of them on top of the table the night before. Aromatherapy, decoration; I don't know. Either way, it was very fitting for the holidays.

"Daddy, do you want to play?" The little man woke up rubbing his eyes as I put him down on the sofa.

"Sure, little man. Just let me help Diana with some things first. That ok with you?"

Jaxon nodded.

"Cool. Would you like to watch some cartoons?"

"Yes, Daddy."

I put on *Paw Patrol*. It seemed to be his favorite cartoon lately. When I went to help Diana, she asked if he was okay.

"He is. He's with us." I grinned and helped her with the groceries then told her I was going to bathe Jaxon while she prepared dinner.

Coming out of the bathroom, the smell of tomato sauce cut through the warm, soapy fog that had gathered. "Smells good, huh, bud?" I asked Jaxon as I dried his hair with a towel.

He nodded enthusiastically. "One more thing, then we'll go eat." I put on his favorite music on my phone, set it on the bed, and started cutting his nails. He loved it. We laughed together as he danced to the beat, his limbs flailing as I wrestled down one foot at a time for cleaning.

"Food's ready!" Diana called from the other room.

Coming out of the bedroom, I could see that Diana had gone all out with the table spread. Probably a wise choice, considering Jaxon did not hold back his appetite.

"Spaghetti, my favorite!" he shouted as he shoved a fork full in his mouth.

Diana and I didn't say much. We just looked at each other and watched him eat himself right to sleep. I woke him up to brush his teeth and fell asleep with him to make sure his monsters didn't come around. My monsters left me alone more often when he was visiting, too. Having Jaxon around just felt right and complete.

The next couple of weeks went by, uneventfully. Christmas came and went with no letters to either refute or remind me that I was considered a dead man.

Just before the New Year, I got a check in the mail for my benefits. They were coming in again! Things were finally looking up for once. Confident that I'd made it over the hardest part, and that the VA was finally working diligently on my case, I started saving my money so I could put a down payment on a car. Buying a car for myself had been in the works for a while, but the death notice from the VA had put my plans on hold indefinitely.

December turned into a cold January. Time flies when life is good.

My next semester was starting in a few days, so I was trying to pick up some overtime until then. I needed to make sure I had enough money for the down payment on the car and enough for the extortionate insurance rates typical of New York City.

Browsing online for an affordable car started taking up all my free time. After what I felt was an appropriate amount of research on my end, I made plans to head over to a used car dealership to check out a couple of cars and finally make a deal.

The dealership was just a few blocks away from home. After a night of tossing and turning in excitement, walking down there would help burn off some nervous energy. On the way out, I decided I couldn't avoid taking a peek in my mailbox. Nothing!

Thank God, I heard Diana say in my head.

At the dealership, I started by walking the lot. No matter how much research you do, and no matter how much you plan your visit, something about car lots made you want to browse. Spotting one of the cars I'd seen the listing for online, I went to take a closer look -- a BMW coupe with low mileage, clean silver paint, and it was in my price range.

My streak of good luck vanished at the most unfortunate time. As the dealer started my paperwork to finance the vehicle, an error showed up on the dealer's screen.

Confusion clouded his eyes, but he immediately called the one-eight-hundred number. He looked at me awkwardly as he listened to the justification for the error on the other end of the line. He asked me for my identification a second time.

The dealer apologized and left to call his manager to sort out my issue. Dressed smartly in a freshly pressed suit, the manager tried taking me through the whole process a second time. He was cordial the entire time, but I could tell that the error was putting him off. He asked to see all the documents I'd brought with me, including my driver's license. I showed him my military ID as well to no avail. He apologized for the error and delivered the bad news.

"You cannot make this purchase, call the credit bureau to clear it up." The manager offered his take with a formal apology, and I left the showroom embarrassed and baffled.

The confused and untrusting stare of the car dealer burned into the back of my head. That was when I realized what had probably happened. His deal had gone stale with a dead man. It was not his fault, but it wasn't mine either.

Numbed by the recurrence of a problem that I thought I'd put behind me, I stood outside the showroom and recorded a play-by-play of the entire incident. Then I dialed the one-eight-hundred number for the credit bureau, hoping that I could nip this problem in the bud. After the usual annoying array of information intake providing my name, birthday, and anything else they could think to ask me, they informed me there was a red flag. She transferred me to their fraud department.

Great. Here we go again.

"Your information matches with our database, but the records declare your status as deceased. We will look into the matter. Thank you for your cooperation." He hung up the call without letting me get another word in.

I knew what the matter was. I could have told him exactly what had gone wrong in their system and pointed them to the VA. Now I was stuck waiting for yet another government entity to clean up the mess they were making of my life.

Thinking back to the clinic months ago, I couldn't help but laugh incredulously at the situation. The same VA department that had failed to update my address change in their records, twice, had somehow managed to permeate my life with obstacles by spreading false updates to who knows how many other departments.

Full of pent up frustration, one little video wasn't enough. I got home and filmed more, documenting the never-ending chronicles of a dead man. Once I was done filming, I reached out to all the lawyers who didn't respond to my messages before, plus a few new ones.

I received some feedback, but nothing substantial. More than anything else, I kept getting forwarded to other people. There were no experts on anything like this, and no one wanted to take on the case themselves. One lawyer even had the audacity to ask me if the situation was real or just a hoax. Crossing his name off my list angrily, I stared blankly at the sheet of paper I'd been using. I was losing hope about this ever getting fixed.

My phone buzzed. "Hey, I just wanted to say I love you," Diana said. I hadn't told her about my problems at the dealership yet.

"I love you too. What's the catch? Are you softening me up for something?" I asked teasingly.

She laughed. "Sometimes, you just need to hear it." Even though she didn't know what was going on, she always had great timing.

While the car dealership had been the only recent casualty in my war against death, its appearance seemed to trigger a flood of other problems. My deceased status was like an infection, spreading through the system and into all the critical parts of my life. The financial department from my MBA program got in touch with me, citing an error on my online F.A.F.S.A form. According to them, I was not going to be cleared financially for the next semester.

Error. Error. Error.

I contacted the financial manager and told her what was going on. She reviewed my documents and told me she would have to get back to me because this was above her paygrade. I continued the semester even though I kept receiving emails that they might drop me from the class. I couldn't afford to fall behind if everything got cleared up soon, and I had nothing to lose by calling their bluff for now. The classes themselves weren't my favorite, but they were a requirement for the MBA program, so I was sticking it out. I got an email from the dean of the program telling me to call his office.

I'd been keeping my phone notifications on so I could stay up to date on any developments, so as soon as I read the email, I called and it went straight to voicemail.

I emailed him back, telling him about the failed attempt and giving him my phone number and good hours to reach me just in case.

I got another letter.

I didn't want to open it.

I just stared at the envelope as it sat on my dining table.

I paced around the apartment, glanced at the table, and then paced some more. Now seemed like a good time for a workout. We're all entitled to run from our problems now and then, right?

I threw on my hat and a light jacket. I could see my breath forming in front of my face as I started a slow jog down the block toward the nearest park. My muscles were fighting to warm up against the chill outside air.

Once my core temperature was high enough that I felt like unzipping my jacket, I turned up the speed. I could feel the adrenaline rushing through my body. The stress didn't exactly melt away, but it didn't rule my thoughts anymore. All that mattered, right now, was the feeling of putting one foot in front of the other, breathing in time with the impact of my heel on the concrete sidewalk.

After about a mile, I picked up the pace again. I was sprinting for as long and as fast as my feet could move. When I couldn't run any longer, I jogged for about a minute, letting my body recover before pushing it to sprint again. I repeated this routine for about half an hour.

After I'd turned my legs to jelly and I couldn't run anymore, I finally decided to head back home. My mouth felt like sandpaper and my lips had a salty taste to them. My lungs were on fire, but it had felt great to get out of my head for a few minutes. The letter was still on the table. Apparently, I didn't run fast enough to escape my troubles.

Taunted by the small white piece of paper, the whole situation came rushing back in, erasing whatever sense of peace I had accomplished.

I need a drink, I told myself.

I walked into the kitchen and poured myself a glass of Jameson Whiskey, sat down at the table, and stared at the letter. I didn't open it.

I checked my email. I even walked downstairs and rechecked the mailbox for something less ominous like spam mail that I could pretend to care about. I opened everything else until that letter was the only thing left staring me in the face. It was from the family court.

I finished my drink in one quick swig and opened the letter. On the top right-hand corner, it said, "For child support." I looked at it in the most confusing way.

I pay child support, I said to myself. *Apparently not enough.* My son's mother was fighting for the child support to increase.

Okay, back to court we go.

Things were getting out of hand, but it could have been a lot worse. Honestly, I wasn't sure what kind of twisted new development I'd expected. If being deceased had somehow released my rights to see my kid, I would have gone ballistic.

A new week rolled around. It had been peaceful for the last few days, but I had come to an understanding that life wasn't going to let me off that easy. I received another email from the dean. Frustratingly, it was just a repeat of his previous request for me to call him. I did, but once again, there was no answer. I emailed him back explaining that I had tried to call him, but that I'd been forced to leave a voicemail.

My phone started to ring as I walked in the door from work. It was the dean.

Here comes my expulsion for being dead or an accusation of fraud, I thought. The anxiety of the call's unknown topic overshadowed any relief I felt from ending our game of email tag.

He asked me if I was interested in law school.

Floored, it took me a second to respond to the non sequitur. "I've been thinking about it, but I'm not too sure yet," I finally replied.

He offered assistance on getting everything together if I decided to head that direction.

I expressed my thanks in as many ways as I could come up with.

He brushed it off and told me to keep up the good work. Then we ended the call.

Wow.

I'd debated bringing up my F.A.F.S.A. problems with him, but it seemed inappropriate. The dean of the college shouldn't be bothered by that kind of thing. That's what his staff were supposed to do, and it wasn't like he'd be able to sort out the real root of the problem, anyway. My status as a dead man was much bigger than one financial assistance form.

I had a child support review the next day, so I took some leave from work and printed out the documents I needed for court. If just one thing was wrong with that paperwork, then it might as well have been toilet paper. I could only hope that my other problems wouldn't rear their ugly heads here.

I got there a respectable thirty minutes early. Jaxon's mother showed up and we went into the courtroom when our names were called. Our Arguments were presented, and we each produced whatever necessary documents demanded of us. After all the paperwork was reviewed, not much had changed. It was decided that we would switch to a bi-weekly payment schedule. There had been a small increase in the amount I would owe going forward, but nothing bank-breaking. I was told to wait for the clerk for further information.

On the way home, I stopped for some more comfort food at a hotdog stand. "Two hotdogs with everything, please."

"That will be four dollars," the man said.

On the way back, I ate like a king. Once my hands were free, I decided to make another video about my struggles. Filming myself had become a staple of my stress-management routine. It helped almost as much as working out. Plus, I'd recently realized I could use it to help others as well. I needed to get my story out, so that anyone else experiencing something similar could point and say, "At least I'm not alone." Maybe they could even use the timeline of my events to head off problems before they happened. It was still just an idea in my head, but it was something.

Diana called me on her lunch break. "Hey, good news," she squealed. "Guess what? The position you wanted to work is finally open."

I'd been gunning for a position in her department for a while. The pay was better than what I currently made, and it came with more benefits. "I will apply right away," I told her enthusiastically.

We spent the rest of the phone call reviewing the child support case, and then I let her go so I could fill out the application as quickly as possible.

Life moved at a steady pace. I heard back from Diana's supervisor with a request for an interview. I continued to save up my benefits money, hoping to be given the opportunity to get that car, eventually. Then another road bomb went off next to the Humvee that was my life.

"What now," I grumbled to myself. The letter was from the IRS. The bolded title section read, "To the estate of C. Rodriguez, please verify he is deceased."

Enclosed were multiple pages of forms and instructions. I quickly ruffled through them, looking for a phone number I could call. Nothing. Where the papers had failed me, the internet prevailed. Dialing the number that *Google* provided, I tried to explain my situation. The customer service agent on the phone was very pleasant but ultimately, she couldn't do anything. She told me I had to go to the IRS office to confirm my identity. She also told me my taxes would be held and an investigator would contact me. *Here we go again.*

On the bright side, this was definitely a new approach. If the government thought that I was playing havoc with their tax money, the investigator was sure to be thorough. More thorough than anyone else that I'd tried to get to help me.

You could be sure that the government would do what they could to label me as alive if it was their money on the line.

With that handled as much as it could be for the moment, I turned my attention to the rest of the mail. Another letter from the school with yet another threat to drop me because my student loans were in limbo. I emailed every relevant department I could think of explaining my situation. Before hitting send, I decided to CC the dean of the master's program as well, even though I'd hesitated to involve him before. I decided it couldn't hurt to keep him updated on something affecting the student he'd decided to sponsor for law school.

My phone rang again. It seemed like my life had devolved into a series of phone calls and letters these days.

Important events or dates with Diana didn't set milestones in my memory, but by, "Oh, that's the week that the IRS called," and "Oh, I got three letters from my college that month," I wearily looked at the unknown number flashing on my phone screen, almost praying that it was telemarketers instead of another round terrible news. Sighing, I picked up the call.

"Am I talking to Mr. C. Rodriguez?" a shrill feminine voice said across the line.

"Yes, this is him. May I ask who this is?

"You recently reached out to us and left a voicemail about a problem you are experiencing with the Veteran's Program, and we are trying to figure out how we can help you." I pumped my fist in the air as she spoke. She was a veteran program advocate.

"If you can just give me a quick explanation about what has happened from the beginning, that would help out a lot," she continued.

Despite being sick and tired of rehashing my ordeal over and over to new people, I explained everything to her with as much detail as I could remember.

"I will advise you to visit the SSI office at your earliest convenience and I'll be in touch with you."

Finally, I thought, *someone who's willing to help me clear this mess up.*

CHAPTER 5

What the Hell is going on? My first night home from deployment was not going the way I thought it would. I'd been looking forward to sleeping in my bed -- an actual mattress, in a temperature-controlled room. It was supposed to be a reward for a long time coming. Instead, I just felt trapped. Everything felt strange like it didn't belong to me. The walls pressed in and the dark was oppressive. I tightly closed my eyes, trying to ignore the feeling and pass out. Suddenly, my throat started feeling constricted. I gripped my shirt in a reflex action, but I was choking on something.

I managed to dial 911, and they sent an ambulance. The bill for that was going to be awful, I knew it, even with insurance, but I didn't trust myself to drive to the emergency room when it felt like I was going to pass out from lack of oxygen at any minute.

They admitted me for "breathing problems" and administered a steroid while they figured out was wrong with me. This had never happened to me before. At first, I was embarrassed. I'd assumed I'd had a panic attack or something, and I'd let it get out of control. The last thing I needed was a doctor telling me it was all in my head.

"Sorry, nothing we can do, but we'll charge you, anyway."

Finally, instead of a nurse, a doctor came in with a clipboard full of interview questions.

"When did you get back?" He asked.

"Just yesterday," I responded.

"Do you have a history of asthma?"

"No, never had any breathing problems before."

"All right, hold tight for a little bit and we'll see what we can come up with." The doctor left the room and came back about twenty minutes later.

"How do you feel?" He asked again in a friendly manner.

"I feel better." I really did, but I couldn't figure out if that was just me or the meds still running through my system.

"We think you might have a bit of anxiety. It happens a lot in recent military returns. We're going to discharge you here, but you should head over to the clinic on base tomorrow for further observation," he said.

Way to go, asshole, I chided myself. I'd called it. One little panic attack and I had to go and embarrass myself in front of a bunch of medical personnel not to mention the hit my bank account was going to take.

"Thanks, doc. I'll do that," I said.

At first, I wasn't even going to bother going in. Why subject myself to even more humiliation if the problem was just me being too anxious? Then I figured, at least I wouldn't be paying for this one. So, I went to sick call first thing the next morning, met up with another doctor, and told him about my episode. He sent me up to the main hospital with a referral.

They asked if I had anything going on for the rest of the day. "Nope."

So, I was admitted for overnight observation. Feeling foolish, I spent the night going through so many testing procedures that it felt like I was being experimented on. One day turned into two when they asked me to stay overnight again.

Later that night, while lying on the hospital bed, it happened again. I couldn't breathe, I couldn't swallow, and my saliva was drowning me. My throat was getting blocked with something. I clawed at my throat, but I couldn't even inhale enough to cough. My whole body had gone rigid as I jerked and spasmed.

Holy fuck... this is where I die. After all the shit I'd been through, I'm going to eat shit to a panic attack.

Somehow during my flailing, I managed to hit the call button over and over. The nurse came in, took maybe half a second to assess the situation, and rushed to my side while calling for a doctor. They pinned me down and started using some suction machine to remove the saliva.

"Relax, Rodriguez," the nurse tried to calm me. Of all things, at that moment, I wished my team commander was there yelling my nickname and ordering me to keep my shit together.

My breathing was still spiraling out of control. They administered an adrenaline shot intravenously and nebulized me. By the time I started to stabilize, my room had become the most popular destination in the hospital. I counted at least three nurses, my original doctor, and another doctor I didn't recognize. Most of them started to filter out when they were no longer needed. One of the nurses stayed behind to check my vitals, assured me that I'd live, and then I was alone again.

The next day, I was told that what I had experienced definitely was not a panic attack. I couldn't decide if I was relieved. Sure, I hadn't been making a big deal out of nothing, but now something was actually wrong with me.

They told me they'd be spending the day giving me allergy shots to see what I was allergic to.

"Why do I have to do this if I have never been allergic to anything except bullshit?"

The male nurse cracked up at my sarcasm, "Me too, brother. But the doc thinks it's best we do this to narrow down anything that could be causing breathing issues. Test for the easy stuff first, then use the process of elimination, and all that shit."

I agreed with the logic and twiddled my thumbs while I waited. We made small talk while he set up the test. He explained to me that he was there as part of his special forces training. We laughed and told war stories. He commented on some of my tattoos, and we compared scars. It was a nice change of pace from the fight or flight panic of the night before.

Everything was finally set up, so they started applying the scratch tests. I broke out with hives right away. My body quickly became covered in blotchy, red blisters. My breathing quickened, and I felt a weight begin to press against my lungs.

They were ready with a shot of adrenaline as I started going into anaphylactic shock. I didn't even feel the needle pierce my skin because I was too distracted by the burning sensation in my chest.

Another nurse ran in with a second dose of adrenaline. Then I blacked out.

My first indication that I was still alive was how sore my throat felt. *If this was Heaven, there's no way I'd have a sore throat, right?* I thought, not bothering to open my eyes yet. *But what if this isn't Heaven? What if Hell is just a void and a permanent sore throat?*

My conscience countered. Typical of me to argue with myself about whether I belonged in Hell or not without even verifying that I'd died. When I finally chose to open my eyes, I was still in my hospital bed. I could barely talk, but I managed to eke out a raspy, "What happened?"

I was told that I had passed out, and considering how awful a lack of oxygen can be, I decided the loss of consciousness was merciful.

After that, I was resigned to an indefinite stay in the hospital while they ran test after test on me.

"You have small holes in your lungs," the doctor finally explained after day four of observation. "Were you exposed to anything while out of the country?"

"I was blown up a few times, but that's it." Only when the words left, my mouth did I realize how messed up it sounded. "EOD once told our team that one of those explosions could have been a chemical bomb, but they weren't too sure," I added, trying to recall the details as much as I could remember.

The doctor took everything I said down and came back in with my blood results about an hour later. According to the labs, some kind of poisonous substances I'd encountered on duty had weakened my immune system to the point that any illness I wasn't already desensitized to would completely trample my body defenses. It hadn't flared up while I was on tour because I'd grown accustomed to everything over there, but being states-side was a different story. They transferred me to an even more sterile room as if I was being quarantined. Over the next few days, I was given shot after shot to help boost my immune system. The meds made my body feel like shit and being isolated didn't help my morale.

I survived the war to die a slow shitty death at home; I thought to myself on a particularly pessimistic day.

My discharge couldn't have come a day sooner. Luckily, I had made it out of the hospital just in time for the military ball. It was great to be back with my brothers. For the first time in my days, I felt normal. Nobody had a clue what I had been through, which was a blessing in disguise because I just wanted to be treated like any other grunt. Even though I was told I would have to be on medication for the rest of my life, I didn't care. Nobody could stop me from doing what I wanted to do with my military career.

I ended up becoming an instructor, training civilians to become soldiers. It was a rewarding job. If I put everything I knew and learned into just one of these soldiers, then it was worth it. While my job was to train soldiers, I also went to college on base. I wanted to work on gaining credit because I was told that I needed college credits to get into Special Forces training. That was my goal.

Long, hard hours of repetitive training honed my body the same way that college honed my mind. When I thought I was ready. I asked my First Sergeant for a transfer to Fort Lewis, Washington.

"Why do you want to transfer? Are you ready for another deployment?"

"Whatever it takes to get me where I want to be," I responded. By the end of the week, I was issued unofficial orders, and about two weeks later, I received official orders with my reporting date. I was getting closer to my goal.

Fort Lewis was supposed to be my last transfer on this side of the Atlantic. I got a promotion while I was there and immediately started reaching out to different special forces group recruiters. I was always packed and ready to go, despite not knowing where I was headed.

"Sergeant Rodriguez, are you sure you're ready to be deployed? You haven't even been home for a full year yet," my superior asked me one evening.

"More than ready, sir. I had no other goals, and no reason to stay here. It was either special services or the front lines of a combat zone.

"All right, soldier, if you say so. Your unit is deploying to Afghanistan."

"Copy that, sir." It wouldn't be professional to get too excited in front of my commanding officer, but I was ready to get back in the fight. As much as I wanted to dive into my special forces training, I also felt compelled to deploy as a team leader because this way, I could continue through my preparatory phases while I was deployed. That's when I hit the first real wall between me and my goals.

"Why not?" I managed to keep "the fuck" out of the middle of my sentence through pure discipline, but the sentence had spiked my temper.

"Your medical history," they said.

I was stuck. I didn't know what to do or what to think. There had to be some way to fix this. Repeating that mantra in my head, I went straight to the commander's office to see what they could do. I'd take any option to salvage my ambitions.

"Sorry Rod, we can't do anything. Stay here and lead from the rear," the commander said.

"Roger that, sir," I said. I wouldn't shed tears in front of my commanding officer, but I'm sure the disappointment and the anger were apparent on my face. Walking out, I clenched my fists over and over and tried not to hit anything.

A few days later, I received a call with orders to report to the hospital the next morning. No explanations, just a voicemail with the time, a place, and a name to ask for upon arrival.

I called my platoon sergeant and told him what was going on. He told me to take care of whatever I needed to do. I assumed it would be something routine and went to bed without giving it another thought.

The next morning, I showed up at oh nine hundred, as ordered. At the front desk, I gave my name and the name of the doctor I was told I'd be meeting. They stuck me in an exam room and left me to chill for a few minutes. When the doctor entered with an all too familiar tray of allergy test kits, my stomach dropped. Why did they need to test this again?

I failed spectacularly, just like I had the first time. My daily meds weren't enough to counteract the acute introduction of symptoms, and I needed an adrenaline shot to help prevent another blackout.

After a day of observation, I was told I was getting medically discharged. I thought my life was over.

Ever since I had entered the military, all I had known was being a soldier. All I'd strived to do was be a part of the elite. I had trained so hard, endured so long, and just like that; I was out. I had nothing else left in life for me.

A lot had changed since those days. I'd found a lot to live for because of Jaxon and Diana. However, now I had to fight for a different set of goals -- namely, the right to continue legally being alive.

Sitting at the kitchen table, procrastinating on my homework for the second hour in a row, I had exhausted myself of refreshing social media over and over to zero new posts. Next step; do the same thing with my email. Then go back to social media and rinse and repeat until I either turned to dust, or I got motivated enough to work. *Oh, I actually* do *have an email*, I realized as I opened my inbox. It was from the veteran program's advocate. I opened it eagerly, hoping to see a plan of action and something to tell me what I had to do next to get this all fixed.

"Dear Mr. Rodriguez, I hope this email finds you well. Unfortunately, because the Veterans Affairs Department has already rectified their internal error and restored your benefits, I'm afraid there is nothing else I can do to help you with your problem. Any improperly filed records or errors from non-VA departments are outside of my ability to provide assistance. I'm sorry you have to go through this, and good luck."

There was that familiar sinking feeling in my stomach. Now I didn't want to do my homework. Opening *Facebook* with the resigned sigh of someone who didn't even find pleasure in their procrastination, I stared blankly at the screen, and that was when I had the lightbulb go on over my head.

I'd already been interested in helping others with my video therapy sessions and sitting here in front of me was a whole audience for those videos, ready and waiting. More importantly, if I got my story out, then maybe it would be seen by someone who could help.

The next day, I set up all of my studio equipment and wrote a script about what had happened up to this point. I trashed and rewrote the script a few times before deciding to send it to a buddy to review.

"Bro, this sucks. Can I make a few changes?" he sent back. I could always count on my friends to not beat around the bush.

"Hell yeah, man," I replied.

It took him less than a day to send back his revised version. It was crisp and hard-hitting. I threw on a button-up and tried my hardest to fix my hair and make myself look presentable. Once I was satisfied with my appearance, I rehearsed my notes and completed a few takes to make sure everything worked appropriately. Sitting in my studio, I'd lost track of time. The next thing I know, Diana was in the doorway watching me work. "Uh, how long have you been standing there?" I asked sheepishly. There was nothing I would be truly embarrassed to do in front of her but sitting in front of the camera and reciting a script had me on edge the same way that public speaking did.

"Not long. What are you doing?" She was enthralled.

"Just playing with an idea." My eyes flickered with excitement.

She smirked, "Here we go with your ideas."

I smiled at her as she turned to leave. "If you need me, I'll be figuring out what we will do for food," she called over her shoulder.

"Okay, love you," I shouted after her.

It took me four hours and a few Red Bulls to edit the final product into something I was confident in showing to Diana.

"What is this?" she asked. True to her word, she'd left me to my own devices, but the suspense was getting to her.

"I decided to take my story public," I said, falling onto the couch with a sense of accomplishment. "People need to see this. What if there is someone out there who has gone through this and can truly help me or that I can help with my experiences? I had to do something."

She looked at me proudly as what I was saying settled in her head. "I think there is a lot you haven't been telling me," she teased.

I sheepishly smiled and showed her all of the phone recordings I had made over time. While most of the events were familiar to her, some weren't, and even the ones she'd eventually learned about usually happened in a way that her involvement came after the recording had already been taken.

She was shocked that I'd been keeping so much from her, especially under the guise of not worrying her. "You shouldn't have tried to deal with all of this alone," she admonished, her words softened by the look of admiration that was still on her face.

I shrugged apologetically, a smile on my face. She knew that I'd promise to do better and that I'd go right back to trying to protect her when it happened again.

Diana watched the whole video, then watched it again. Afterward, she asked if I could change a few things. She wanted the videos to portray an educated, intellectual kind of veteran seeking guidance and raising awareness.

As a result, I shaved my face, changed into a different button-up shirt that she picked out, and had her help in conquering my unruly hair. I looked professional but relatable. I went back into my studio for one more take and spent the next day piecing it together in an editing program.

After Diana got home from work the next day, I presented her with the new final copy.

"You clean up pretty good," she teased before continuing, "and your message is very powerful. Are you ready for the level of attention this is going to bring?"

"Any amount of attention is good attention," I replied. "If all I do is react to things as they go wrong instead of getting proactive, I'll never fix this."

She smiled at my determination. "I know. Once you set your eyes on something, there is no stopping you." She kissed me on the forehead and went to take her post-work shower while I put some finishing touches on the editing.

Satisfied with the product I'd created with her help, I sent it out to a few of my friends who knew about my story. They were blown away.

"Holy crap, this is nuts," one of my friends sent via text. I decided to wait until I got out of work before I posted the video on social media. If I sent it out in the middle of the night, it might not gain enough traction before other posts sent it into the depths of people's feeds.

First, I uploaded it on *YouTube*. Then I linked the video to *Facebook* and uploaded a small clip-on *Instagram* for good measure. Nothing happened for about a day. Views trickled in, but I kept telling myself that just because viral content was spontaneous didn't mean it was always immediate. My waiting paid off the next morning. Out of nowhere, my video started gaining traction. It jumped from 12,000 views to 28,000 in under an hour. Someone popular must have linked it to their followers because it was starting to spread. Everyone who watched it started sharing it with their own social media groups.

Then, suddenly, my video disappeared from *YouTube*.

I tried calling their customer service about it but only got automated services. So, I did the only thing I could think to do and reposted it. Every time I uploaded it, I got an error. My video followed the community guidelines, so I couldn't understand what was wrong. I hadn't even monetized it. Getting attention was more important than ad revenue.

Finally, after battling with the automated systems for a couple of hours, the original video resurfaced. No explanation, no hint as to why it had been removed in the first place, but the views were intact, and the ability to share it had returned, so I decided not to waste too much time wondering why it had glitched out.

The video's momentum continued to build exponentially. I got my first call for a radio talk show the next day.

"Hey, this is Dave from *Veterans Take Charge Radio Show*. Our show found your situation interesting and would like to talk more about it."

I told them I'd be happy to appear on the show and to create awareness around my situation. With my explosion in popularity, one of my friends decided I needed my own website as well. Things were finally going in a steady direction.

CHAPTER 6

After my discharge, I felt aimless. Before I'd gotten out of the service, I had been accepted to Penn State University, but all I'd ever known was being a soldier. Could I really switch tracks and pursue a degree as a civie that easily?

It wasn't like I had much say in the matter. Even if I disagreed, I couldn't exactly tell the military, "No thanks, I don't feel like being discharged. Take me back."

Dejected but resigned to my fate, I drove from Washington State to Pennsylvania to begin my new life. It was a long haul, about forty hours of driving, alone providing me with enough time to think, but not enough to figure anything out.

I never realized how different I'd become. The lack of emotion was a clear as day. Nothing phased me anymore. I could sit still and silent for the abnormally long stretch of hours. I'd drink to suppress the demons and quiet the nightmares, but I found no joy in being drunk.

I fought and argued with everyone around me, and going to bed angry became my routine.

The little girl, the beautiful five-year-old girl I had forgotten in the dunes of time, came to me, "Mista, Mista, please help me," she pleaded, her voice squeaky and bird-like.

Despite the obvious cues, I wondered if I was asleep. I felt so awake. Is this real? I could feel the breeze, and everything was so detailed. People say you can't smell anything in a dream, but I could. Bleach and blood and smoked gun powder filled my nostrils. I was frozen in place.

She turned her back toward me and started to walk away.

I can't move. I want to reach out, to hold her, to protect her. "Let me help you!" I shout.

She stopped. At first, I was hopeful. She heard me! She's going to let me help. Then she turned, and the bullet hole once again marred her face. I cry out, and suddenly she's in my arms. I'm kneeling, covered in her blood. This isn't a dream. This is Hell.

The dreams never really went away, but I found that the more stress I was under, the more often I'd wake up in a cold sweat, reaching out to try to help someone who'd died in the desert years ago. Once I'd figured that out, I tried to come up with ways to reduce my stress.

Given my lifelong commitment to the military, it wasn't long before I thought that the perfect solution to my lifestyle problems was to re-enlist.

"You're a code four, bro," the recruiter said. "There is no way for you ever to get back in unless the draft comes back."

I was told most guys try to go back too after a few weeks of getting out. I guess I was no exception.

I would wake up now and then in my combat boots, standing in the middle of the room with my sweatpants still on. My drinking habit worsened. At some point, I started bringing women home with me. None of them ever stayed longer than one night. Being woken up by a guy screaming bloody murder in his sleep next to you will do that.

One night, my nightmare dragged me to a deserted road. I could feel the blood oozing out of my ears as a bomb exploded right beside my truck. I could hear the tinny sound of someone reporting through the headpiece in my helmet, "Contact, contact! Truck two, unable to move. No survivors. We will have to blow the truck up on site." I started yelling with everything I had "I'm alive, I'm right here!" No one heard me. They gave the grid of my location as I continued to scream. The sound of air support boomed overhead, followed by a blast. Flame and metal screamed through the cabin, shredding me to pieces as smoke and blood filled my nostrils.

I fell out of bed, startled and screaming like a maniac, my skin clammy and profusely sweating. When I was able to make sense of my surroundings, I realized I had been sleeping beside a woman.

"You need to see a shrink," she commented, clutching the bedsheets to her chest.

I apologized, but it fell on deaf ears as she dressed and left in the middle of the night. Apparently, I was becoming a danger to myself and others.

I started spending more time with family and less time out at night on the race strip. Being around family helped stabilize me emotionally. They helped me try to feel things other than anger and anxiety. However, no matter how much recovery I was making while I was awake, my nightmares would not leave me. She came to me again. Sometimes I reached out, but I was always a few inches from grabbing her hand. Other times I was frozen able to shout but not to move. She brushed the hair off her face, and it was my niece screaming for help. I could hear her crying and coughing, but I could not save her.

I started walking to the niece's room to confirm she was safe in the middle of the night. Months had gone by without a single night of a sound sleep. I was physically and mentally at a rock bottom.

My schooling suffered as well.

Lectures were not engaging enough to keep me awake, but not relaxing enough to give me the sleep I desperately needed. With hooded eyes, I would lay my head on my desk and zone out.

"If anyone wants to sleep in my class, they can just leave," the professor announced one day after I'd failed to respond to a question, he'd directed at me.

I wanted to sleep, but I couldn't, so I resorted back to drinking. I realized I needed help when I woke up days later in my own home. I found myself naked on the balcony reeking of alcohol and my vomit. Everywhere I looked around me were bottles of vodka, but I could not remember a single moment of that week.

I headed to the VA hospital, smelling like a bar. I was admitted and was placed on a few IVs. I was asked if I was interested in meeting a few people who had been in the same place mentally that I was. I said sure. I was given a referral to some group meetings for Vets. Honestly, it helped. I ended up meeting a ton of friends whom I can call family to this day.

The veteran group's meet-ups gave me a space to share my guilt and my traumas. Everyone there had their own little girl. Except in some cases, it was a little boy, or a friend, or a squad mate. They understood everything I shared. I was able to sleep for once.

***

"We're going out for dinner. Let's do Chinese," Diana announced as soon as she reached home. I was never one to deny a good plan. So we ended up in a Chinese restaurant followed by a walk along the Verrazano bridge. We talked endlessly about our school, about Jaxon, and everything else that was going on in our lives. As we reached our building, I took a package I'd hidden away in our mailbox and handed it over to Diana.

"What is it?" she asked curiously as we got into the elevator.

"It's for you," I winked.

She laughed and shook the box. Finally, she started peeling away at the packaging to reveal a small turtle-shaped ring. Placing it on her ring finger, she extended her arm to admire it.

"I know I'm always worried about stressing you out because you lead such a high tempo life. So whenever you're losing your mind, or I'm being a stubborn ass about something, just focus on the ring. You'll calm down." I looked at her and tried to resist breaking out in a teasing grin.

She giggled and kissed me, "How thoughtful of you, babe."

Back in the apartment, I did a quick check-up on my email and my website. Despite the momentum, my videos hadn't been able to entice an attorney to handle my case.

Most of the comments were well wishes or appreciation for taking the time to share my story.

It was a chilly but bright day as we took the subway to work together. I gave her a goodbye kiss and went to my department to get my daily assignment. Everything started off great. I was feeling productive and making good progress on what I needed to get done that day. I was daydreaming about sending Diana a message asking what she wanted for dinner when I got my hand smashed into a door.

Cursing under my breath, I groaned thinking I'd avoided bullets and bombs to get my hand destroyed by a damn door in the heat of the moment; it didn't hurt much. However, once the adrenaline wore off, and the swelling kicked in, it was obvious that I needed to see a doctor. I was sent to the emergency room. Luckily, the x-rays came out fine; they bandaged my hand and sent me on my way along with a small supply of pain meds. As I got out of the hospital, I saw that I had twenty missed calls from Diana.

"Will there ever be a day when you will let me in on the action?" She sounded pissed. "I can't believe you made me hear about this from one of our coworkers before you told me yourself."

I could not hold back my chuckle despite the unbearable pain.

"Babe, I am perfectly all right, I promise. Don't forget to look at your ring."

The growl that emanated from the other side of the line would have made my drill instructors piss their pants. "Kidding! I'm kidding! But really, I'm okay. I swear."

"...Fine," she said after a short, angry silence. "Just go home and ice it."

Properly chastised, I dutifully took the rest of the day off to nurse my hand and work on some of my videos. Editing with one hand was a pain in the ass, but producing fresh content was important. Plus, I'd go crazy if I had to sit at home doing absolutely nothing.

Since I had enough time on my hands, I called the SSI office and spoke with a customer service rep who made an appointment for me to come in and talk to them about my legal zombie status.

I also called the DMV to see if my license had been suspended or revoked. The lady at the help desk said I would have to come in and confirm who I am before she could tell me anything one way or the other. Trying to remain proactive without leaving the apartment, I sat down and made a list of all the agencies who have possibly been notified that I was dead. What stared back at me, much to my dismay, was almost every single agency there was. *Well, I'm sure the Department of Energy couldn't care less if there's one less carbon footprint in the world. But that doesn't make the rest of this list any less annoying.*

I woke up the next morning to my hand twice the size it should have been and throbbing like crazy. Popping some of my pain meds, I unwrapped the ace bandage to reveal a purplish, bruised mess. It looked crazy.

Diana gave it one look, winced, and said, "You know you're going to the hospital, right?"

"Yeah, I know. The last time I went down there, though, the wait was awful. So first, I'm going to try the doctor's office across the street."

Satisfied with my compromise, Diana kissed me on the forehead before heading out the door for work. True to my word, I finished getting ready and then jogged across the street to visit the local clinic. I rang the buzzer, and they let me in. After the receptionist saw the size of my hand, she didn't bother waiting for me to finish unwrapping the bandage to reveal the bruising. I had an appointment for the next day.

Calling in a sick day, I headed back home and reached out to some friends so I could get their feedback on my videos. A good friend from Texas replied, "Bro, this is crazy. I'm glad you're doing this, though. People don't really understand the struggles of veterans."

I agreed with him; I was a firsthand witness of that.

From there, we small-talked about family and life. I told him he should come to visit for a while. After we wrapped up our call, I tried getting ahold of Trish, a friend from college who was now a screenwriter in Los Angeles. I wanted her expert opinion on my videos.

"I have seen every single one of them. As a veteran, I think your situation is insane. I always keep you in my prayers. Anyway, I showed your vlog to a few people out here and the vets out here seem to be curious. Many people thought it was fake until you started showing real documents then their doubt turned into 'Oh man this is crazy.' If I get any hits working out here, I will definitely drop your information."

Trish was a non-stop talking machine like always. As I ended the call with her, I made a mental note of her advice. "When you make the videos show who you really are. Show your life and how you really live. People want to see a personality behind what's going on."

I started reviewing all the videos and decided to change the way I was filming. I made it more entertaining by adding a personal touch. I had tons of spare footage of parties, friends, and family time. Even videos of Diana and I just shooting the shit and hanging out in the apartment. It was fun to edit and piece the footage into a narrative. As I played after the final cut, my video had a very refreshing feel to it; I was thrilled with the outcome.

I was early for my doctor's appointment the next day. Living across the street from the doctor's office had its perks. Plus I wanted to make sure I had plenty of time for paperwork before my appointment time since I'd be filling it all out one-handed. Unfortunately, my preparedness did not translate into good news from the doctor. They'd taken some X-rays, and the results were less than promising.

"Mr. Rodriguez you've messed up your hand bad," He looked at me through his glasses, "Two broken bones in the thumb and a ligament tear."

I winced, this sounded like a recipe for elongated rest.

"I'm going to prescribe you some medication, and you need rest. Forty-five days without stressing it, at least. Then we'll revisit and see how it's healing."

Called it. Why am I so good at predicting bad things? I thanked him for his time and left the office with a slip of paper for the pharmacist. First things first, I needed to call my department to inform them of the injury.

"Okay, send us your paperwork, and I guess you'll be on leave for forty-five days. We'll cover any expenses for the injury. Just make sure you get better. Good luck."

My supervisor was really cooperative. I sighed, relieved. My old position might have just let me go on the spot if I asked for that much time off.

The next order of business was calling Diana to let her in on the action; she appreciated my obedience.

"Anyway, what are you going to do with all of your free time since you can't go to work or the gym?" She teased me.

101

"I guess I'll spend most of it editing, and maybe doing some outreach for phone interviews or something," I said. You could almost hear the pout in my voice; it was difficult for me to live without gym time.

"Cheer up big boy, how about we go to Puerto Rico for like a week?" Diana suggested. She was plotting something.

"I'm all ears," I chuckled.

"Well, I'm glad you agreed because I am already scouring cheap flight tickets." She hung up the call with a laugh.

It was still early, so I decided while I was waiting for my prescription to get filled, I could visit the IRS office to see if I could speak with someone. I filmed my trip there, taking the time to point out landmarks, both famous and personal, before putting the camera away as I approached the building.

"Good afternoon, I would like some assistance about a case." I was buzzing with optimism.

"Well, do you have an appointment?" The clerk looked at me as I if was dumb.

I shook my head no, undeterred by her judging stare.

"Make an appointment first." She handed me a card and picked up her phone before staring at me as if to say, "I'm busy; please go away."

I walked out and called the one-eight-hundred number hoping I could make an appointment right then and there.

"Sir, the next available appointment is three weeks from now. That's the standard wait time for the NYC area."

I booked the closest appointment time I could. My next destination was to the SSI office, which ended up being no dice, too. It's not like it was a holiday or something. Why did some government buildings keep such weird hours? Nothing I could do about it now, I supposed. Grabbing my new medication, I headed for home while mentally planning out the content of my next video.

CHAPTER 7

I have said before that I'm not a pessimist. Some people might call me out on that, pointing out how I was quick to complain when the shit piled on. Even in my memoirs, there should be plenty of evidence of times that I've felt demoralized, miserable, and cynical, but none of that made me a pessimist, at least not in my eyes. It was all about context.

Despite a neglected childhood and a troubled youth, I never thought life wasn't worth living. I didn't give up. When I managed to find a sense of purpose in the military, everything just got better. Even where most people would consider rock bottom, I had just been waiting for that opportunity. Optimism, to me, was about drive. It was about goals. So what if I bitched and moaned along the way, as long as I put one foot in front of the other?

***

"Are you ready to fight for your country?" the sergeant's voice roared.

We roared back like a pack of lions in drill formation, ready to take the fight to our enemy.

"Let's move! Go, go, go!" A different sergeant this time, accompanied by the sound of explosions in the background.

"Requesting fire support, danger close! We are pinned down!"

"Get on that fucking gun, Hot Rod!"

"Fuck, I'm hit!"

***

The voices followed me everywhere. The military had discharged me, but I couldn't figure out how to make the break mutual and stop caring about it. Alcohol was becoming less and less effective, but that just made me drink more and more.

I'd been at emotional lows like this before, but that had been when I was in the military. The structure and the belonging carried me when everything else in my life had been falling apart around me.

"Enough is enough, Carmelo Rodriguez. You have to decide," Trisha's sharp tone hammered at my patience while my barely one-year-old son cried at the top of his lungs. I hated it when she used my full name like that. Like I was some immature child in need of discipline when she was the one throwing a tantrum.

"Could you keep your voice down? You're scaring Jaxon," I said. Putting enough anger in my voice to stand up for myself was hard when I was trying to calm down my son simultaneously.

"Stop using him as a shield and quit avoiding the subject!" she snapped.

I wanted to yell. Being accused of using Jaxon for anything as petty as leverage during a fight infuriated me. "I'm not avoiding anything. You knew what you signed up for when you said yes to marrying me," I said coldly.

Had we rushed into marriage too early? Everybody hears horror stories about couples who get married at eighteen, but it's always, "Not us, though. We're the exception."

We were so sure that we were soulmates. My commitment to the military had already been an accepted part of my life, and we both were okay with that, or so I thought.

Problems started right after my first deployment. She pushed for me to quit as soon as I was able. I wanted to go career in the military. This wasn't a new decision. My goal had always been to stick with the military for as long as they'd have me. However, she didn't want to be a military wife. I don't know what kind of expectations she'd had, but apparently this wasn't living up to them. Then we had Jaxon. He was the light of our lives; a bundle of joy that made us forget all our problems for a while. However, a baby is not a solution to an unhappy marriage.

"Carmelo, are you even listening to what I am saying?" Trisha's voice pulled me back to the present.

"Trish, please understand. I can't do what you're asking of me," I said helplessly. "Being a soldier is the only thing that I know. It's the only thing that's ever made sense to me."

"Being a good husband doesn't make sense to you?" she retorted. "I don't care how much you love the military. I don't want to be a military wife."

The finality of her tone told me that she had already made up her mind. This wasn't an argument anymore, it was just a serving of emotional divorce papers.

Eventually, those became actual divorce papers, too.

Now, sitting in the dark with bloodshot eyes and alcohol on my breath, I couldn't help but feel bitter. I'd let the military tear my family apart, only to get kicked out because of a fucking allergy. My support system was gone. I was continually relapsing and driving away anyone close enough to help me. It was one of the shittiest parts of an objectively less than ideal life, but that doesn't make me a pessimist.

***

"Babe, did you put the sunscreen in my purse?" Diana called out from the bathroom.

I was on the laptop in the kitchen, trying to run through some last-minute edits for my latest video. Our flight to Puerto Rico was in four hours, and I didn't want to be forced to upload a day later than I'd planned.

"Not yet. I'll get to it in a second," I shouted, my eyes not leaving the computer screen.

She appeared in the doorway to give me an exasperated look.

I'd packed the night before, but one look at my single piece of luggage left her unsatisfied. Now she was in the process of rearranging everything, getting herself ready, and generally running around like a chicken with her head cut off. *Or a boot officer leading his squad for the first time*, I thought with amusement.

"It's fine, I've got it," she said. "How much longer are you going to be glued to that? Have you showered? I don't want to sit next to a stinky boyfriend on the plane."

I knew she meant well, so I just laughed. "Not much longer, I promise." If I was being honest with myself, I wasn't sure that the trip to Puerto Rico was the best idea right now. We could afford it, sure, but with my life, in

107

limbo, like it was, it felt frivolous. Plus, what if some critical development happened while we were on vacation? I'd debated bringing these up with Diana, but I felt like she needed this trip, and to be honest, despite my reservations, I could probably use it too.

As we reached the airport, we passed through security pretty quickly and settled in the waiting lounge.

"Hey, you wanna grab a burger? I think I'm hungry," I asked Diana as I spotted someone leaving one of the terminal restaurants with food in hand.

"Nah, I am going on a diet," she sighed.

Unable to contain my immediate reaction, I let out a short burst of laughter. "Why are you going on a diet? You look fine." I'd never thought Diana would be the kind of person to be overly conscious of her body.

She huffed. "You didn't see me trying on my swimsuit before I packed it."

Seeing that she was serious, I leaned in to kiss her on the cheek. "Well, I think you're gorgeous. But I'll support you if that's what you want to do. Just don't make me eat rabbit food the entire time we're on vacation. That defeats the purpose of letting loose!"

We shared a laugh as the terminal began calling for passengers to board. We stood and filed into the forming line. Staring at the back of her head, I wondered what karmically amazing thing I had done.

The flight was completely uneventful just the way I liked it. As we landed in Puerto Rico, Diana and I decided to grab a quick bite from a cafe located near our hotel.

"I love the vibe of this place," Diana gushed as the waiter served our dishes.

"Yeah, Babe, it's great," I replied absentmindedly. I didn't mean to be dismissive of her attempt at conversation, but something had caught my eye. A group of young US soldiers was passing by, distinct from the crowd in their uniforms. It wasn't precisely jealousy that tightened in my gut, but a sense of acute loss. I didn't blame them for being able to serve but having the fact that I would probably never be able to join them again still stung.

"Hey, are you all right?" Diana asked, placing her hand on mine.

I pulled my eyes away from the group. "Yeah... yeah, I'm fine. Let's eat." Turning my full attention to the empanadas in front of me, I spent the rest of the meal, making small talk about the architecture of the buildings around us and the quaint aesthetic of the neighborhood.

After finishing our dinner and a small round of dessert. "But, I'm still on a diet!" Diana pointed out we headed to explore the beaches.

Hand in hand, we walked barefoot through the sand along the shore. My mood had been steadily improving as the evening progressed, and I decided that maybe I needed this trip more than I'd thought.

"So, you never talk about what I just witnessed at the cafe," Diana suddenly asked, looking up at my face to assess my reaction. She was never one to hold back her curiosity.

"What do you mean?"

"You know. Sometimes you'll go someplace else in your head," she said. Her curiosity was genuine, but when I look back at the moment, I realized she was trying to get me to talk for my benefit more than hers.

I rubbed the back of her hand with my thumb while I thought about what I wanted to say. "It just bothers me, I guess. To see other people serving when I can't."

She nodded thoughtfully, then asked, "Do you hate the military for discharging you?"

"Hate them? No, not at all! It wouldn't make much sense for me to hate them and want to rejoin them at the same time. If I hate anything, it's myself. Me and my body's inability to hack it," I said, trying not to get too emotional. Talking about it out loud was harder than I thought it would be.

"You can't blame yourself for that!" she scolded me gently. "You wouldn't blame someone with cancer for having it, would you? No double standards because you hold yourself up to some kind of higher bar."

My health was a tender area for Diana. She was always so worried about me, and I knew that I often didn't make that easy on her.

"All right," I conceded, "I see your point."

"Yeah, you better!" she suddenly smirked as she jabbed me in the rib with one pointed finger.

Making an exaggerated surprised face, I said, "Oh, you're going to get it!"

She laughed and danced away from me, running down the beach before turning to taunt me, "Only if you can catch me!"

CHAPTER 8

Despite struggling to adjust to college and life as a civilian, Penn State was instrumental in helping motivate me to move forward. At the time, it felt like I was being pulled along, attending because I had been accepted, but aimless in what I wanted to do with that education. One of my professors saw this, and I remember the first time she approached me to give me a goal.

"Rodriguez, you should write more. You have a real talent for it," she once told me as she handed me an assignment. I smiled and thanked her, taking her compliment as a formality, not reading too much into it. A week later, she approached me again.

"So, Rodriguez! Have you written anything new?"

I was taken aback. "Umm, no Professor Johnson. I'm not really a writer," I said, shrugging. I was comfortable writing essays for my classes, but I'd never considered it something I should be doing in my free time.

"Here's the thing, Rodriguez. You have the talent to take this somewhere," she gestured for me to follow her as she walked. "I'm sure you're thinking that I'm just trying to encourage you because you're my student but trust me. I read hundreds of essays from college-educated people every year. I know actual talent when I see it."

"I'm not so sure, professor." I don't know why I was so hesitant to accept what she was saying. One of the first things the military instills is confidence. Maybe I wasn't ready to have an ambition again. The wound from aiming for the special forces was still raw, but she was insistent.

"Let's make a deal," she said. "There is an upcoming event for creative writing pieces. If you submit something and perform it, you don't have to attend my class for the rest of the semester, and I'll give you a passing grade."

My eyebrows raised in astonishment. If I even submitted a piece, I'd pass her class? Not "if you win" or "if I like it," but just "write it and perform it." It had to be too good to be true.

I expressed as much to her, and she wagged a finger at me. "You think I'd joke with you, Mr. Rodriguez?" she admonished.

"All right, Professor, you've got a deal."

Finding inspiration proved to be more difficult than I'd expected. Being promised a passing grade just for participating seemed to have a counterintuitive effect on my ability to produce work. Even though I could have written anything, I wanted to make the piece worth the grade.

The first spoken poem I wrote resulted from my frustration over the trivializing attitudes of people around me. Sitting at a cafe staring at a blank word document, a conversation between a group of young millennials caught my attention.

"Seriously, I don't get people who join the military. Who looks at a career of volunteering to go kill people and get involved in countries where we don't belong and decides that's what they want to do with their lives?" One of them said with derision.

It was ironic that while living in a college town, I could run into so many uneducated people or at least when it came to things that they had no experience. I wanted to go over to his table and start listing the names of all of my friends who had died so that he could freely speak his skewed opinions. I wanted to find a way to put him in my shoes, to show him what being a soldier entailed and why people chose to do it.

That's when I realized I could do those things. Maybe not in the way I'd initially envisioned. If I approached him and his group, he would probably blow me off. I'd be labeled and judged before I could even make my case. However, maybe I could express myself on paper.

Inspired, I spent the next hour typing furiously. Each word needed to make an impact, and I probably erased six or seven drafts worth before I settled on something I was satisfied with delivering.

The event wasn't for another week, but I already knew this would be the piece that I would submit.

It felt strange to look forward to something again. I still wasn't exactly sure where my life was going, but, at least in the short term, I had a goal. When they called my name, and I walked to the podium, looking out over that crowd of people, I knew that I was experiencing an important event in my life. Even if I never decided to pursue writing seriously, I needed to be able to express myself. Clearing my throat, I looked down at my poem and began.

"This piece is about America. About our love affair with war and guns, but also respect and responsibility. It might sting, but I hope I can get across the message I'm trying to impart."

And, then, I read my poem.

I am our nation's hero.
A skeleton hidden in your grandfather's
nightmares.
Birthed in 1969 by the U. S. military,
An M-16-A1 rifle is what I'm named.
Rambo called me the true American Badass,
Standing at thirty-nine point five inches,
Weighing a little over seven pounds fully loaded.
I'm in your children's cartoons, you kid's
Christmas gifts
I came here to warn you,
I follow my leader's directions as he grips my body
and pulls the trigger.
I'm what our country talks about.
The sight of my shells ejecting from feeding
chambers spreads like bloodshed
Throughout history for the glory of our waving
flag.
I matter.
The second amendment keeps me alive, &
Your forefathers made sure of that
I've created borders, enriched our economy
enforced security
Society looks down on me because
I've flooded so many cities with tears
While being prejudiced is not in my vocabulary,
I'm not made for clumsy hands.
Soldiers trust me and keep me close because I am a
son's fate
A wife's lifeline
A husband's true love
The hug me holding me tight at night

Hoping I won't jam when the time is right
See cuz this ain't Hollywood
It's far from a movie.
When on safe I'm silent and cold, yet,
I can still make any neighborhood sound like the
fourth of July
Forcing mothers to cry as I paint flesh like a bull's
eyes
And remember,
While I'm used for war mayhem
I attend every service man's funeral.
Twenty-one shot in one class
You know why?
Because my America,
My America loves me.

The conference hall burst into applause as I stepped back from the podium. Stunned by the reception, I wasn't sure whether to wave, take a bow, or walk back to my seat. Eventually, the event organizer came out and gestured for me to leave the stage, which I gratefully did. People smiled and continued to give me small gestures of praise as I passed their seats to take my own.

After everyone else had finished presenting, and the event had ended, Professor Johnson approached me. "That was a very thought-provoking piece, Mr. Rodriguez," she said. Her attitude gave me a distinct *I told you could do it* vibe.

"Thanks, Professor. If it wasn't for you, I probably never would have given writing a serious shot, I told her earnestly."

"Maybe I gave you a little push, but you put in the work. Now don't stop. I'll be very disappointed if that ends up being the only written piece, I ever get to experience from you."

"I won't, professor. I promise," I assured her. "Oh, and one more thing. You'll be seeing me in class tomorrow."

She smiled knowingly. We both knew that there was no chance that I'd want to miss her class, no matter what our deal had been.

From that day onward, I realized that while my demons would always stay with me, and I wasn't resigned to a silent suffering. Writing became an outlet to express my deepest thoughts and allowed me to finally start feeling like I was a part of society again.

***

The week we spent in Puerto Rico was fantastic. Good food, beautiful sights, and no responsibilities were the perfect recipe for a boosted morale. I napped through most of the flight home, and Diana made sure to tease me for the fact that at one point, I snored loud enough for the entire plane to hear me.

Back in dreary reality, New York hadn't changed a bit in our absence. Leaving the airport was a hassle of traffic and bad drivers. Eventually, we made it home without incident, but it was a revolving door for Diana. She had a training program in Virginia that she was required to attend, so I'd be getting the apartment to myself for the next week.

"Don't just sit at home in your boxers all week," she admonished as she went through her luggage, swapping vacation clothes for business casual.

"I won't, I promise."

"I mean it. Go grocery shopping at some point. Don't just order takeout every night. And go to your doctor's appointment."

I just smiled and patted her shoulder. It never felt like she was nagging me when she got in one of these moods. It probably had something to do with the fact that I knew she was doing it because she cared. There's a world of difference in hearing someone fret over you because they love you, and hearing someone order you around because they think they know what's best.

"I'll miss you," she said as she finished packing.

"I'll miss you too," I replied. "Don't worry, Babe, it's only a week. I promise the apartment will still be standing when you get back."

She gave me a quick kiss on the lips, and she was out the door.

I spent the afternoon brainstorming ideas for a new video. I'd allowed myself the luxury of not worrying about anything while we were on vacation, but I didn't want to let myself get too lazy now that I was back. Thinking about my situation made me realize that we hadn't checked the mail since we'd gotten back. My mood soured a little at the thought of having to go through the backlog for the week, especially if there happened to be any hidden landmines among the spam.

My anxieties were confirmed when I pulled a letter from my bank out from between two coupon flyers. Apparently, there were issues with my records. It didn't take a genius to predict what kind of problems they might be. Sighing, I pulled out my phone to call the bank's customer service line. As much as I hated the robotic menus I had to navigate, it beat going down there in person and waiting in line.

When I finally reached a live person, I went through my usual spiel. I gave them all the information they needed to confirm my identity and then asked them what the problem with my account was. I was fully prepared to explain the legal mess of my unfortunate demise to the customer service agent, but instead of getting a chance, they put me on hold. After about ten minutes listening to a loop of what amounted to upbeat elevator music, the agent came back on the line.

"Mr. Rodriguez?" she asked.

Uh oh, I know that tone, I thought. "Yes? Can you tell me what the problem with my account is now?"

"Actually, we need you to visit your nearest bank branch before we can discuss any further details."

"Why can't we talk about it over the phone? I can't really make time to go to the bank today." That wasn't entirely true, but it was more like I didn't want to have to go in.

"It's just a formality, but we do need you to come in. Since it's Friday, please come by on Monday if at all possible," she said.

Sighing, I agreed to try; and make time to visit. There wasn't any point in arguing with her about it, and I doubt she had the power to fix my complaints even if I voiced them.

Once I'd finished talking with the bank, I decided to update Diana on the situation since I knew she'd be irritated if I didn't. She probably wouldn't be able to check her phone for a few hours, but I left her a video message with all the pertinent details and a promise to follow up first thing on Monday.

Even though I had shirked visiting the bank, I decided that sitting at home was a bad idea. I'd just come back from vacation, and I could already feel the gloom of dealing with my situation settling over me. *Maybe I'll get a burger.* Even though it was technically take-out food, Diana had only specified that I couldn't have it every night, not that I couldn't have it at all. Secure in my loophole logic, I grabbed a jacket and started walking down to the nearest fast food place.

After devouring a quarter pound of beef with more cheese and bacon than you could imagine, my mood was satisfactorily improved. I walked back out of the building, the smell of grease and condiments wafting after me into the evening air. My phone buzzed. *Must be Diana returning my video message*, I thought, but when I glanced at the screen, I saw that it was my old buddy Jeff calling.

"Hey man, what's up?" I asked.

"Hey, Rod, I was calling to see if you're available tonight. Bunch of us are going out for drinks," he said.

It had been a while since I'd caught up with him, and it would be great to see some of the other guys too. "Hell yeah, Diana is out of the city, so I am totally idle at the moment."

"Awesome. See you there in half an hour? The usual place."

I confirmed the details, and we ended the call. Jeff and I had never served together, but we'd met at a memorial service for a close mutual friend who'd died in Iraq sometime after I had been discharged. It hurt thinking that I could have maybe been there for him; that things could have been different if I was still in the service. Jeff had understood that kind of guilt, and we bonded over it.

We swapped contact info, and he invited me to a poker game at his place about a month later. His friends were all cool dudes, and everyone swapped war stories all night. Since then, I've considered Jeff and his group to be my surrogate squad. Maybe I couldn't serve anymore, but I still needed that connection with people that understood all the shit that only other military guys could.

Knowing that I'd catch a lot of shit if I showed up late, I took the subway instead of walking. It was Friday night, so the bar was packed. Our regular table was in the back corner. It always amused me that we could secure that spot no matter how busy the place was.

"About time, soldier," said Christina, an ex-navy officer, and the only brass in the group.

"Grunt Rodriguez, reporting, Captain," I said humorously while the rest of the group chuckled.

Jeff, Thomas, and Sam were all grunts like me while Christina and Dominique were both squids. Each of them had seen their fair share of action. All retired. Some by choice, others had been pushed out like me.

"What's everybody been up to?" I asked as I took a seat. "How's the leg, Jeff?"

"Hurts like a bitch when it rains, but therapy is going about as good as can be expected," Jeff said as he flagged down the bartender.

As he ordered a round of drinks, one of the other members spoke up. "So Rod, they're calling you a dead man now?" Thomas asked, his brows furrowed.

I sighed as the whole group looked at me with sympathy. "Can we put back at least a couple of rounds before I start with the depressing details," I requested.

The group assented, and everyone else went around the table taking turns catching everyone up on their own lives and problems. Despite the generally cheery atmosphere, you could tell nobody wanted to bitch and moan as much as they usually did, though. They didn't want to seem like they were whining over insignificant shit when I'd obviously drawn the short stick for the past couple of months.

Three rounds of beer and one round of whiskey later, the topic finally turned back to me.

"We've all been worried. I follow your vlogs religiously, hoping that one time you'll get on there and tell everybody they can stand down and that everything is fixed," Christina admitted as she tore into a buffalo wing.

"You're not the only one wishing for that day," I said, acting nonchalant. "The problem isn't even the VA anymore. They started this shitstorm, sure. But now it's like a frag. The initial explosion kicked up all this shrapnel, and I'm stuck trying to find just how many pieces hit something important."

"That's fucked up, man. Like... you're standing in front of them with all these proofs of identity. What more do they want?" Jeff shook his head with disdain.

"The system is fubar," Dominique pitched in. "It takes five seconds to fuck your life up, but five years to put it back together again." She gave me a look that said, *Well, hopefully not five* years.

Everyone pitched in their agreement to her statement, then fell silent for a moment. It was a comfortable silence, filled with eating, drinking, and enjoying each other's company. We understood just how shitty the universe could be but stood together in spite of it.

"So, how are you feeling about it all?" Thomas's question broke the silence. It was the one I wanted to avoid, but we all knew it would get asked, eventually. Each one of us understood the consequences of disturbing events on our emotions and feelings.

"Well, if I'm being honest, pretty shitty. Right now, I'm okay. And I have good days. But realizing that the VA fixing their mistake wasn't the end of it was kind of a punch to the gut. I'm just always waiting for another piece of mail or another phone call to tell me what new part of my life is getting destroyed. It's demoralizing as Hell."

Everyone nodded in understanding. This wasn't the kind of thing you fixed with empty words, and they all knew that.

Thomas slapped me on the shoulder as he handed me another drink. "We've all got your back, man. Now enough doom and gloom shit. Those two girls at the bar have been checking you out all night."

I looked to my left, and sure enough, two attractive girls were taking turns looking my way and giggling to each other.

"Ugh, it's the tats," Sam commented jealously. "They always fall for the tats."

"It's because girls like a bad boy," Christina said playfully.

"I could be a bad boy," Sam pouted.

"Sure you could, bud," Jeff said teasingly.

Everyone laughed, and we finished up our last round of drinks. It was getting late, and we were all pretty buzzed at that point, so we decided to call it a night.

***

The beeping of my phone woke me the next morning. I'd slept through my first two alarms, and apparently, I'd somehow managed to snooze this one without remembering. *Shit, I missed my meds*, I realized.

Grabbing the pill bottle off the bedside counter, I staggered to the kitchen for a glass of water. *God's a real dick for inventing hangovers*, I mused through my headache.

Despite Diana's lecture about not spending all my time in the apartment, I elected to stay inside today. After managing to make myself a decent breakfast, I sat down in front of the laptop. I wanted to start creating a buffer of extra videos in case there were times when I couldn't take the time to make a regular upload. Other veterans had begun reaching out to me, and many civilians had been leaving supportive comments on the series. Keeping a consistent schedule ensured that I wouldn't lose that momentum and with it, my chance at finding people who could help me.

I'd missed a call from Diana while I was asleep, but she'd left me a video message afterward. Her training schedule meant she would be busy all day, but she wanted me to know that she'd gotten my message about the bank. She reminded me to take my meds and told me that she loved me. Smiling, I took the time to send her a message back before concentrating on my videos.

Sunday, I decided I would go grocery shopping so that I could stop skirting around Diana's orders. We'd purposefully used up most of our spoilable food before leaving for vacation, so the fridge was looking pretty bare. I grabbed eggs, milk, a loaf of bread, and some fresh fruits to snack on. When I got to the checkout line, the cashier greeted me with a friendly smile. I came here often, so he recognized me and said, "Haven't seen you around in a little bit. Been busy?"

"Yeah, I was actually out of town on vacation for a week, just got back a couple of days ago."

As he finished ringing me up, I put my card in the chip reader. It beeped an error at me.

"Looks like it declined," the cashier commented. "But it might just be acting up. You can try again?"

A second attempt yielded the same result. Pulling a second card out of my wallet, I tried that one -- same thing. "That's weird. One second, let me see if I've got enough cash."

After counting it out, I had enough for the milk and the bread, but not the fruit or the eggs.

"It's fine, just take it. You can pay me back next time you come in," the cashier offered.

It was generous of him, but I didn't like the idea of taking charity I didn't absolutely need. Fruit could wait another day.

"That's all right. Thanks, anyway, though. I'll see you again once I get this all sorted out, hopefully."

After leaving the grocery store with my meager half-bag of food, I decided to stop by an ATM. I was officially cash poor, and if my cards weren't working, I was going to have trouble for the rest of the week to eat until Diana came home. When I tried to access my account, however, the ATM screen showed another error. *Uh oh*, I thought. I'd already promised Diana that I would follow up with the bank on Monday about that letter, but now I had an extra incentive.

The next morning, I left home at 9:00 a.m. sharp. I wanted to work out the bank situation before it got any more messed up than it already was. I took the subway and in an hour, I was in the city. It was another fifteen minutes' walk from the subway station to the bank, and the whole time I could feel my heart sinking lower with each step and a queasy feeling in the pit of my stomach. I was not in a good place for another piece of bad news. I reached the bank and immediately asked for a manager.

The employee behind the counter didn't know who I was, but he decided that helping me had not yet reached the appropriate level where he needed to involve management. Instead, I was directed to another employee in one of the small cubicles that lined one wall of the lobby. Usually reserved for people who needed to discuss private details at length, such as taking out a loan or opening an account, there was thankfully no line.

"All right, sir, how can I help you today?" he asked courteously.

"I got a piece of mail on Friday telling me that there were problems with my account. I called your customer service, and the woman told me I needed to come in, and it couldn't be fixed over the phone. Then, yesterday, my debit and my credit card were both declined, but I know I have money in my account," I said, barely taking time to breathe between grievances.

"Well, that sounds like quite an ordeal. I'm sure we can help you sort this whole thing out, and I'm sorry that you were inconvenienced. Can I have your account details, please?"

He was a poster child of politeness, but it irritated me a little that I felt like he was reading his responses off a training card.

After supplying him with my account number, my full name, the last four digits of my social security, correctly answering my secret question, and providing him with both my driver's license and my military ID, he took a minute to stare at his computer screen. Then back at me. Then back to his screen. "One second, sir. I'm going to go get a manager to help you further."

If my eyes could have rolled any farther into the back of my head, I probably would have been able to see my brain.

"Sir, your account has been suspended because there appears to be some fraudulent activity," a manager told me a few minutes later. He was looking at me with that all too familiar face that said, "Are you really who you say you are?"

"What does that mean? Has someone else been using my card? I keep a pretty close eye on my statements, and I never saw any suspicious charges before you guys froze my shit."

Normally, I didn't cuss in professional settings, but this was getting on my nerves. I needed for him to come out and tell me that they suspended my account because they thought I was a dead man. I didn't have time for this song and dance routine, especially when it had happened a million times already.

"Sir, I'm not sure I'm allowed to discuss the details of this account with you until I can further verify that you are, in fact, the owner," the manager replied.

"Oh, for fuck's sake," I said, losing my temper. "You think I'm dead, right? That's what this is about? You think Carmelo Rodriguez is dead and I'm some kind of super conman that can fake multiple forms of IDs and I've come to fraudulently steal the pittance of money that's been saved in that account."

The manager started to stammer a reply, but I cut him off. "I'm Carmelo Rodriguez. This isn't some huge scam. The VA, God bless America, decided to tell everyone I was dead, and now I'm busy running around trying to get you, the IRS, and everybody else to give me back my shit. You can call them right now, and they'll tell you I'm telling the truth. At least, they will if you can actually get through to a real, competent person in something resembling a reasonable timeframe, but I'm going to go out on a limb and say that's not likely."

"Sir, I understand you're upset, but even if what you're saying is true, there isn't anything we can do about it without more proof. If you could send us some kind of notarized letter, maybe..."

"Fine," I said. I was done bothering with these people. "I'll come back when I have more proof. But you can bet your ass that as soon as I get access to my accounts, I'm going to switch banks to someone that will give a shit about their customers instead of feeding them cue cards." I was making a scene, but I didn't care. I could physically feel the anger boiling off of me as I turned to leave.

I made it maybe ten steps out the door when I collapsed onto the sidewalk. A younger guy, maybe twenty at most, saw me go down and quickly kneeled to check on me. "Dude, are you all right?" he asked. "Are you sick or something? You're burning up."

I wobbled unsteadily to my feet. "I'm fine," I said. "Thanks."

He didn't look convinced, but he didn't try to stop me when I started walking again. After an agonizing walk back to the subway station, I managed to make my way home without kissing the concrete a second time.

To say it was an unlucky day would be an understatement since the elevator was closed with a board that said, "UNDER MAINTENANCE." I kicked at the elevator door furiously and winced sharply, instantly regretting that decision. I climbed the stairs to the fourth floor short of breath and panting and sat right outside my door for a few seconds to find the strength to unlock the door and enter.

I slumped on the couch, indecisive about what to do next. I knew laying like a dead-meat would not help, but I felt like shit. My head was pounding, and the room was spinning like a damn machine. I managed to pull myself over to the sink for some water, guzzling it down while I stood in front of the sink. Once I couldn't drink anymore, I stumbled toward the bedroom and let myself fall face-first on top of the covers. Hours later, the sharp ring of my phone roused me from my impromptu nap.

The sun had already set outside the window, and I realized it was a lot later than I'd intended for it to be when I woke up. The phone rang again, and I patted my pockets, but I couldn't find it. It must have fallen off the bed somewhere. After getting down on my hands and knees, I spotted it as it lit up the bottom of the bed with its screen. *How the fuck did you get under there,* I thought as I reached for it.

The caller ID flashed Trisha's name. I groaned, contemplating whether to pick up the phone. I did not have the energy to deal with any more conflict right now. However, it had been weeks since I had talked or met with Jaxon. Praying that she was in a decent mood and that this wasn't a call to harp about increased child support, I hit "accept."

"Daddy!" Hearing Jaxon's voice on the other side of the line was a pleasant surprise.

"Hey, champ! How are you?" I asked, clearing my throat as I tried to sound energetic despite feeling like crap.

"I'm fine. Meet me! I wanna the amusement park with you." Jaxon could tell his stories in broken words pretty amazingly, or it's just a parents' thing that we understand everything our kids want to convey.

"We'll do that very soon, champ," I replied, letting the sound of his voice replace my negative feelings. He kept talking for a good ten minutes while I just listened peacefully.

"Honey, you've talked enough. Let me talk with your daddy," I heard Trisha in the background talking to Jaxon in a very motherly tone. Trisha was no doubt a great mom, which was the truth despite our differences.

"Hello, are you there?" She asked, hearing silence from my side.

"Yeah, I'm here."

"Jaxon really wants to see you," she said.

"I want to see him, too," I replied. This was a surprisingly civil conversation for us.

"Good. Let me know when you can come get him. Are you all right? You don't sound so good."

There was no point in complaining to her about my illness. It wasn't like she'd be genuinely concerned by any health problems I was having unless it affected my income. Still, it was strange for her even to ask, and to let me choose when to get Jaxon, instead of setting a time for me and demanding I accommodate it, was strange as well. Realizing that I'd just stayed silent on the line while I'd been thinking, I told her I was fine, and that I'd get back to her soon to let her know when I could come to pick up my son.

After hanging up the call, I headed for the kitchen. I didn't have any cash, access to my cards, or food beyond what was already in the fridge. *Well, at least I'm not technically breaking Diana's rules and subsisting off of take-out since I can't afford take-out,* I thought sarcastically.

After making myself a peanut butter and jelly sandwich, which was the most complicated meal I still had the ingredients to make, I popped another pill and returned to bed to pass out.

The next three days and nights were constant torture. I could not get a good night's sleep for an hour. My nightmares were back, and I couldn't decide if their increased frequency was because Diana wasn't here, or because I was sick. All I knew was that the gruesome images kept flashing through my eyes, the blast of rifle shots, the explosions... I lived through everything again and again for the next three nights. My temperature would continuously fluctuate. I ultimately finished the meds, but refilling my prescription required a copayment that I didn't have. My hand hurt like Hell. Those three days I spent without real food, surviving on bread, condiments, and beers, tossing and turning in fitful snatches of sleep.

Stuck in a dark room and suffocating, I screamed and kicked, shouting for help. "Somebody, help me!" I banged on the walls. They sounded like wood and felt like satin. I was in a coffin. "Get me out of here!" I screamed with such ferocious intensity that I could feel the taste of blood in my throat, and I gagged.

"Babe?" I heard a voice, a very familiar voice from somewhere outside the coffin.

"Help me," I begged that voice for help. I felt someone slap me on my cheeks, asking me to open my eyes.

I struggled to comply, but suddenly, I could feel someone holding my hand. I looked back to find the young girl with a bullet wound covering her face. "Don't leave me alone. I'm hurt," she said in a sweet, pleading tone.

I wanted to stay. I wanted to help her, somehow. "Don't go," she asked again, her face oozing out blood. The sight made me gag again.

Suddenly, a cold blast of water pulled me back to reality. I blinked as my eyes adjusted to the sudden light, and I saw Diana staring at me with horror in her eyes.

"Don't faint on me again," she said, holding back tears.

"What day is it?" I grumbled in a heavy voice that sounded foreign to me.

"It's Friday morning. Can you get up and walk to the bathroom?" Diana asked.

I suddenly realized I was covered in a pool of my own vomit. The gagging in the dream wasn't just a hallucination; it was actually me vomiting. Shit. With Diana's help, I managed to stand unsteadily. "I'll clean myself up," I told her, trying to put on a show of bravado.

"If you need any help, let me know," she said, letting me exert my stubborn independence.

Warm water cascaded down my body as I stood in the shower, fully clothed. Once I felt like I'd gotten a majority of the mess off, I stripped down to finish showering. I left the wet clothes in the tub and walked back out into the bedroom, where Diana was waiting with a clean pair of pants and a shirt.

The smell of carpet cleaner lingered in the air. She'd cleaned up after me while I was washing off. Once I dressed, she silently grabbed my hand and led me to the dining table. Sitting me down in front of a bowl of hot soup, she spooned fed me without saying anything.

"You want to go and lay down on the bed?" She asked me once I'd finished the bowl.

"No, I'm fine, I'll just sit on the couch," I managed in my hoarse voice.

"Whenever you feel a bit more energized, let me know," she added, "we'll go to the doctor."

Normally I'd expect her to be throwing a very justified tantrum right about now, but she just sat there silently.

"What made you torture yourself like that?" she finally said clutching my hand tightly in hers.

"Why didn't you reach out to somebody? You had my emergency number. You have so many friends. Hell, even Trisha is in New York. Anyone of us could have been there for you."

I closed my eyes tightly not to let the tears spill. Soldiers do not cry; I reminded myself, but then something whispered inside of me, "You are a human being, even before you were a soldier."

I remembered Diana telling me not to hold myself to a higher standard than I'd expect of anyone else in my situation.

"I was tired of all this shit, and this constant humiliation." I pinched the bridge of my nose to hold in my tears, but it was too much. Each word was punctuated by short sobs that I couldn't stop.

"Let it all out," she whispered, and I broke down for the first time in a very long time. I was too exhausted and too broken to even care about anything at that point.

Diana held my injured hand before I could it hit it on the table and held me. She cried right along with me as I narrated her how and what happened throughout the week during her absence. I could see my pain reflecting in her eyes.

"I so want to sue them for the emotional and physical distress that their one careless mistake is causing you," she hissed under her breath, making me smile at her concern. "Stop smiling! I got so scared to see you in that condition," she said wiping her tears off before turning to dry mine. I'd never really thought about suing the VA, or anyone really, over what had happened to me. I was too busy trying to get them to acknowledge their mistakes, even to consider punishing them.

"Let's go to the doctor now," she suddenly ordered. There was the Diana I was used to seeing. I wanted to object, to put it off for tomorrow, but I knew I wouldn't win that fight in a million years.

As she was helping me with my coat, she asked, "So, is that what it was like when you came back from the military?" She was definitely indicating the condition she found me in earlier.

I sighed. "No, it was worse than that. This is nothing compared to that time," I said, and she drew a sharp breath as the reality of my words hit her.

The doctor looked at my hand, and then back up at me with a disappointed look on his face I'm sure he was thinking some pretty choice words in his head, but he held them back out of professional obligations. "Mr. Rodriguez, you've certainly tried your hardest to make a mess of your healing process," he admonished. "But the good news is that you didn't do any permanent damage. I'm going to give you an IV to replenish some of your fluids and write you a new prescription. Please remember to take this one."

His tone was firm but understanding. He must have seen something in my eyes; knew somehow that I didn't need a lecturing. I thanked him and lay back on the bed while Diana squeezed my free hand. Once he'd left the room, she turned to me and furrowed her brow sternly.

"That's the last time you pulled something like that off." She said in a very threatening tone.

"I promise, I won't," I whispered back, intertwining her fingers in mine.

CHAPTER 9

Once I had completed a year at Penn State, I'd decided it was time for a move. I was doing quite well in my studies; more than I ever imagined I would. Going through rehabilitation and support groups specially designed for veterans, I eventually realized there was still a life that had to go on. I had two options -- either to give in to destroy myself dealing with the past, or find other ways to make my life purposeful, rejoice in the past and find optimism and positivity in the present. I chose the latter.

One of the driving factors that lead me to move to New York City was my motivation to play a more active role in Jaxon's upbringing. I did not want to be an absentee father who'd visit his son once or twice a year. At first, Trisha did not agree and fought against making any arrangements; however, eventually, after going through a custody case and child support, I was able to have visitation rights to Jaxon.

"I'll not be intrusive at all. I only want to be a part of my son's life," I promised. I'm not sure whether she believed me, but my intentions were clear, and I meant it, making it easier for me to adjust to the academic environment.

Once I'd managed to acquire a job, things began falling into place. My studies continued at a respectable pace, and I was the active father I'd always wanted to be. I was finally at a good place in my life, with great friends and my child. I was living and enjoying the perks of bachelor life.

Work during the weekdays plus classes took up my time, but I had the weekends to myself. Every alternate weekend Jaxon would join me while during the others I'd hang out with friends or workout insanely in the gym.

"Dude, you'll die single, if you don't hook up with someone," Jeff once said as we met for drinks. The crazy thing was that everyone agreed with him.

"No need to gang up on me," I said, pulling a face. "I simply don't want the hassle of relationships for now. I'm living the good life."

"Are you sure? I could hook you up with one of my friends," Christina teased.

"God, no. Anybody who would be friends with you would definitely be too much of a handful for me," I retorted.

Putting on a mock-shocked face, Christina mimed getting stabbed through the heart. "You're ruthless," she said. "See if I ever offer to do something nice for you again."

I just laughed. "You're not some hotshot who can get any lady he wants, you know," she continued. "I know you think you'll be able to turn on the charm once you feel like settling down, but you're not irresistible. I have a friend whom I know for a fact doesn't like you."

"Sounds like a challenge," Thomas quipped, bumping me with his elbow. "Are you going to let her question your Casanova capabilities like that, Carmelo?"

"First of all, no more alliterations in public, it's embarrassing," I ribbed, "Second, I don't feel the need to rise to such petty bait."

"Oh, come on," Jeff exclaimed. "Don't be such a puss."

The conversation continued on that trend for the next ten minutes before the group found something else to distract them. A few months later, Christina invited all of us to her place for lunch.

"Love what you've done with the place, Christina. A total revamp," came a silky, soothing voice from somewhere behind me.

Intrigued as to the source, I turned to see who had spoken. A woman in a black dress stood with her back to me. There was something about her that caught my attention. Sam noticed my gaze linger and winked at me. I smiled sheepishly and raised the glass to my lips.

The girl went toward the backyard to join the group of ladies already seated. Despite my discrete attempts, I couldn't catch a glimpse of her face. Giving up, I turned to begin mingling again when Christina approached from another room. "I hope my husband didn't bore you guys with his business talk," she said to Sam and me.

"I like your husband more than you, so maybe he should be the one apologizing," I teased her.

"Oh yeah, smart ass?" she retorted, hitting me on the arm. The men laughed.

Christina's husband was a very good-natured man, and we'd met him a few times before already.

"Christina, who's that girl in the black dress? I think Carmelo wants to be introduced," Sam said with a mischievous glint in his eyes.

Christina looked at me a bit surprised and then burst into laughter. "You like that girl?" She asked, still laughing like a lunatic while I rolled my eyes at her.

"Sam's crazy; it's nothing like that. I couldn't even see her face."

"Well, she's facing the window right now. Take a look. She gestured toward the window where the girl stood with her friends.

Damn, she was beautiful, I thought. She'd squint her light brown eyes every time she laughed, and there was this warm glow about her personality, which was attractive.

"Oh, her name's Diana. And, did I mention she's the same girl I told you about?"

I looked at Christina, with confusion. "The one who doesn't like you much," Christina said.

The whole group of men in the living room burst into laughter as my face turned red with embarrassment.

"Sam, you are dead meat," was all I could quip. My darling friends were undoubtedly enjoying every moment of it.

"Dude, we really feel for you right now," Jeff said, trying and failing to contain his laughter, he put on a supportive face.

"Come on, Rod! I think you can win her heart," Thomas encouraged. "Christina's always full of shit, anyway. Maybe this Diana girl does like you."

"Hey!" Christina said in a mock-hurt voice.

I'd stopped paying attention to their teasing. Thomas's last words kept echoing in my head. Maybe I did have a chance?

"Come on guys, time to flip burgers," Christina said, holding back her laughter and winked at me mischievously.

I ran my hands across my hair and joined everyone outside, trying to put on an air of calm, relaxed confidence. Christina put me in charge of grilling duty, but I didn't mind. I was a maestro at cooking meat, and it gave me something to do to distract myself from the girl in the black dress. Music played on the speakers, and the sound of laughter and conversation filled the air as groups of people mingled across the lawn and at various tables. Call me boring but getting to sip on a beer and watch it all play out without having to participate was my idea of an ideal get together.

"You need some help with that?" The soothing honeyed voice from earlier called out.

Almost dropping my spatula, I turned to see that Diana had somehow snuck up on me. *Smooth move, Butterfingers.* "Nah, I'm fine," I said. "You should go and enjoy the party."

"I'd like to help, anyway," she said and smiled.

Ugh, she seems like the kind of person who likes to get her way, I thought as she stepped up to join me at the grill.

"I'm Diana, by the way." Before I could introduce myself, she continued, "And you're Carmelo Rodriguez, ex-US army."

She extended her hands toward me and I obliged, "That's right, although I won't ask how you know that."

"Well, you can, if your meat turns out better than mine," she chuckled and threw her head back to put her blonde shoulder-length hair in a bun.

"Challenge accepted. If you were trying to give me a hard objective, though, you should have picked something else," I boasted with pride.

"We'll see Sergeant," she laughed and flipped one side of meat while I tackled the other.

Christina emerged from the kitchen carrying salad bowls and spotted us laughing. "Well, you two are getting along quite well." Having successfully stirred the pot, she then retreated while Diana ducked her head to hide her smile.

"Whatever that was," I muttered under my breath, trying to act like I didn't know Christina's ulterior motive.

"Well, that was a taunt," Diana replied, straightforwardly. "She tried to hook me up with you for a date once, but let's just say I wasn't sold on the idea," She said a tad sheepishly, biting the corner of her lower lips.

This girl doesn't beat around the bush, does she? "The part where you admit that you don't like me very much comes after that, right?" I laughed while her face turned a pretty shade of pink.

"Oh my god, she told you that?" She covered her mouth with her hands and immediately looked around to make sure no one saw her embarrassed face. She was safe because everyone was busy with their chores and chatter.

She's adorable.

"All right let me clear the air. It's not that I dislike you. I just thought you looked kind of arrogant when I saw your picture on her phone."

"Arrogant, huh? I know that's not a compliment, but I guess I'm glad you don't dislike me, at least," I said. Instead of my normal teasing tone, however, I'd delivered the line with all the seriousness and moping of a rejected puppy dog. *I deserve an Oscar*; I thought when I saw her wince, convinced that I'd meant it the way I said it.

"Oh my god, I didn't mean it like that! How do I make this right?" she squished her face between the palms of her hand.

I bent down a little to peer between her fingers into her eyes. "How about you say yes to a coffee date with me? That might make me feel better."

She heard me with confusion in her eyes, and then when she finally understood what I meant, her eyes popped open and lips parted with surprise until she realized I was putting up an act.

"Definitely arrogant," she declared, faking a wounded stance over my deception.

"You can't know I wasn't serious unless you get to know me," I retorted, putting on my most innocent, convincing face.

"...Fine, let me give you my number. Text me when and where, but don't expect a second date if you're not absolutely the most interesting man I've ever met," she warned.

I just smiled. *Challenge accepted.*

***

"Babe, you should be resting," Diana tried to snatch the laptop away as I sat up in bed, scrolling through social media. It was a lazy Sunday morning, and I was in much better condition compared to the dreadful last week.

"Nah, I'm good. Don't worry." I said. My laughter proved my point, so instead of trying to wrestle it away from me, she sat on the edge of the bed and peeked over my shoulder.

"What are you doing?"

"Christina just shared an old album on *Facebook*, so I'm reliving the memories," I told her.

"Which one?"

"The one where you did not like me very much. The barbecue party." I chuckled while Diana rolled her eyes at me.

"You will never let me live that down, will you?"

"Never," I replied and laughed again. It felt good to laugh.

"All right, stop reminiscing and get up. I'm starving. Let's go get breakfast."

"So, what's on your agenda tomorrow?" she asked as she stabbed at a large stack of pancakes. "I guess your appointment with IRS is approaching soon, right?"

"Yeah. I'm going to get the VA to give me some documents so I can visit the bank first, though. I don't want to have to be worrying about carrying cash with me everywhere while I'm fighting this thing," I said.

Mentioning the bank caused Diana's face to cloud over with a worried expression for just a moment. She smoothed it over almost instantly, but I was so familiar with her mannerisms that I'd noticed it, anyway.

"It's all right, Babe," I assured her. "I'm not going to let them get to me like they did last time."

I would not be one of the twenty-two veterans who took their lives every day.

That's true; twenty-two veterans die because of suicide every single day in the US, but this veteran was going to fight the fight until the very end.

I braced myself for one last battle.

CHAPTER 10

A bead of sweat rolled down my temple, muscles tensed as I fought to crawl out of the overturned Humvee. Smoke stung my eyes. Heat emanated from a small fire that had caught one of the tires. I could feel it pulsing in waves as it flickered and ate at the rubber.

Suddenly, I was back in my apartment. Another nightmare, but something had woken me up. Usually, that didn't happen until I was screaming and tossing and turning. I felt a weight press against my chest, and I realized Jaxon was lying on top of me with his small arms wrapped around my chest. He'd taken it upon himself to become my pressure blanket, protecting me from my demons with his embrace.

I could feel the rise and fall of his chest against mine as his small breaths warmed my skin. Stretching slowly, I curled my arms around him in a hug and held him tightly. I was confident that I wouldn't have any more nightmares when I let myself drift back to sleep. At least, not while I had Jaxon here with me.

"Get up, Jax," I tickled Jaxon, rousing him from his sleep hours later. Diana had left early for work, leaving Jaxon and me to sleep in together.

"Hi Dad," he said, yawning, and then he opened his eyes wide. "I am hungry."

Barely awake for two seconds and the first thing on his mind is food. He's definitely starting to take after Diana, I thought humorously. "All right, champ. Let's get you cleaned up first, and then I'll cook?"

"Yeah!"

He giggled as I bundled him up in my arms and dashed toward the restroom. After supervising him brushing his teeth, I led him back out toward the living room. "Go play with your toys on the couch, bud, and I'll whip us up some tasty waffles," I told him.

"Waffles!"

I smiled at the way he could make his one-word responses express so much. As I popped the first set of waffles into the toaster, my phone buzzed on the counter. Picking it up, I checked the caller ID. It was Diana. "How are you doing, Babe?" I asked her, pleased to hear the happiness in my voice.

"Just bogged with work. I wanted to call and make sure you guys were getting up some time before noon. You must be enjoying your time at home." Her tone was teasing, but I could tell she was secretly pouting.

"Hey, you're always getting on me about my sulking, so you better quit it!" I admonished lovingly. "When you get off work, I promise we'll all do something fun together."

"Deal!" she exclaimed before hanging up the call. I smiled again. Diana's eating habits may have rubbed off on

143

Jaxon, but it seemed his one-word replies had rubbed off on her in return.

After breakfast, I let Jaxon go back to his toys while I grabbed my laptop from the studio and brought it out to the living room to work and keep an eye on him. My inbox was overflowing with replies from different lawyers, some sympathizing with my situation, but most turning down any consultation as being way out of their expertise. Disappointment momentarily washed over me, but I only had to glance over at my son as he blissfully played with his trucks and his army men to regain my resolve.

Filming the progress of my case had hit a wall too. Between my mangled hand and the financial problems at the bank, I hadn't been able to find time to make a video. *Well, there's no time better than the present*, I thought to myself. Sure, Jaxon was making explosion sounds with his mouth and acting how a rambunctious young child would be expected to behave, but that didn't stop me. If I was trying to humanize my videos, letting him play in the background might even help my case. I wouldn't put him on camera; I didn't want to feel like I was exploiting my son for my videos but making a point to showcase the fact that I was a father and a caregiver as well as a vet might help me get taken seriously. Heading back into my studio, I grabbed some of the more mobile equipment that I could use to film in the living room.

I set up the lights, turned on the camera, adjusted the tripod, and inhaled deeply. *Showtime.*

Living through the experiences that I was portraying was not easy. Filming myself talking about it was even harder. When I made spontaneous videos out on the street, it was therapeutic, but having to contain my emotions and deliver a professional, helpful vlog for people took its toll. It was a conscious decision not to burden people with the depression that I struggled with as part of my situation. That didn't mean that I hid the negative aspects, of course. The whole damn thing was a negative aspect, for the most part, but no matter how shitty and messed up my life got at times, I made a promise to myself not to cry in front of the camera. Given the turbulent nature of recent weeks, I thought I was going to struggle not to break that rule, but having Jaxon there soothed my emotions.

Carmelo getting ready to record his Vlog.

Editing this one was a breeze. I didn't feel the need to splice in any clips of my life since I felt like the sounds of my son and the casual backdrop of my living room spoke for themselves. An hour later, it was ready to go online. As soon as I posted the video, the comments started rolling in. People were horrified to realize that I had suffered for a whole week without any cash or food. Over the course of the next hour, I started getting tons of emails from news sites and other media outlets. It would take me hours, maybe even the whole weekend, to sort through it.

"Wake up, honey," I heard Diana say from somewhere overhead. Blinking the sleepiness out of my eyes, I squinted as I realized that she was hovering over me. I was sprawled on the couch, and I realized that I must have dozed off.

"Shit! What time is it?" I started to scramble, worried that I'd lost track of time. Realizing that Jaxon's still sleeping form was on top of me, however, I quit struggling.

"It's all right; it isn't too late," Diana reassured me. "It's pretty unusual to come home to you napping your afternoon away, though," she commented. "Normally, you're glued to the laptop or letting Jaxon wrestle you into submission."

I chuckled at the mental image of my little man, scrambling on top of me and pretending to pin me down. "Yeah, I guess today was just a little bit exhausting. Maybe I'm getting old." I needed to tell her about my latest video and all of the media outreach we'd received, but it could wait.

Extracting myself out from underneath my son, I headed to the shower while Diana helped him get up and comb his unruly bedhead. We decided to take Jaxon out for dinner rather than staying in. Holding my son's hand in my right, with Diana on my left, I felt more complete than I had in a long time.

The restaurant was relatively calm for a weekend night. Sitting in a corner booth, I ordered a burger and fries while Diana had some vegetarian taco bowl, and Jaxon made excited gasping sounds when he realized they had chicken fingers. "I decided to put up a new video today," I told Diana as our food arrived.

"Oh? This is your first video since… I got back from my training trip, right?"

I could tell what that pause had inferred. She meant to say, "Since I found you in a pile of your own vomit," but we were both trying to move past remembering that point of weakness in my life.

"Yeah. I got a pretty huge reception to it, too. I'm probably going to be getting in touch with the Senator's office," I announced, slathering my fries in ketchup.

Diana rolled her eyes. She thought I was joking. "Sure, Mr. Bigshot. Are you hiring a secretary now as well, since you've become so internet famous?" she teased, making a grab for one of my fries.

"I mean it!" I said. "A couple of news outlets emailed me, asking for an interview. If I do them, I'm hoping it will give me enough weight to ask the Senator for a meeting. I want to advocate for all the other vets that are probably suffering through the same thing I am right now."

I pulled out my phone to show her the emails.

Her eyes widened as she began scrolling my inbox. "A couple? There are so many emails here," she said, impressed.

I cleared my throat, giving her an admonishing look when she met my gaze.

"All right, fine," she said after a short staring contest, "I concede. I'm sorry for making fun of you for thinking you had a bigger head than you actually do."

"Do I have a big head?" Jaxon piped in, placing his hands on his cheeks.

Diana and I looked at each other and then burst out into laughter.

When I talked about doing news interviews and making videos, I always made sure that everyone knew my priority. It wasn't about fame, and it wasn't about trying to make a quick buck. It was about trying to help people and to spread awareness, but it was also about moments like these. I needed my life back so that I could keep being as happy as I was in that corner booth.

Sample of Carmelo's T-shirts.

CHAPTER 11

The next couple of days flew by. Vlog updates took up a considerable amount of my time when you added together filming, editing, and social media management. If I had been doing this as a career, instead of in a last-ditch effort to save myself from legal limbo, I probably would have considered hiring someone to help at this point. As it was, all I could do was try to multitask to cut down on how long I spent doing anything. It didn't help that I had a regular job to attend to, as well, or that I needed to continue contacting every department and agency I could to nag them into fixing something. The issue with IRS was still pending, my semester payments were stuck, and any financial agencies I'd interacted with were after me trying to figure out if I was committing identity fraud.

I'd just finished editing my latest vlog when I noticed a recent comment under a previous video. The commenter had wished me good luck in my struggles and mentioned how he understood my predicament since he was a victim of a mistake by the VA as well.

Carmelo's Vlog during an editing session.

This was my first time interacting with someone else who'd gone through the same thing as me. Did he ever resolve his issues? Could he help me fix mine? Or maybe was it the other way around, and was he a fresh casualty of the VA's negligence, and I would have to be the experienced advice-giver. Either way, I needed to speak with him and learn more. "Can we talk on the phone or meet in person if you're close to NYC?" I asked via private message.

The reply came almost immediately.

"I am open to the idea of meeting you, Mr. Rodriguez. I am attaching my address since I can't travel much due to my illness," he said.

"Do you want me to drive you?" Diana offered later that night over dinner. I'd been so excited to tell her about my encounter that I hadn't even thought about how I was going to get there.

"No, Babe, that's all right," I said after a moment's consideration. "It's not that far, and I could use the excuse to stretch my legs. The subway is less frustrating than traffic, anyway."

The next morning I hit the gym for my usual cardio workout before getting ready to head off to meet with Mr. Johnson. A queasy feeling developed in the pit of my stomach as I made my way down to the subway station. Meeting with someone who was suffering through the same things I was should have been an occasion to celebrate, so I couldn't figure out why I was so anxious. Maybe, I feared that he'd tell me it was something he was still dealing with after ten years. I couldn't handle the thought of being confronted with knowing there was no relief in sight for me.

Thoughts of anxiety combated with the hundreds of questions I wanted to ask raced through my brain, occupying me all the way to his doorstep. Realizing that I'd arrived at my destination, I double-checked the address to make sure that my autopilot hadn't steered me wrong. *This is the place.* As I rang the doorbell, a man in his fifties who sat in a wheelchair opened the door.

"Hi, I am…"

Before I could even finish introducing myself, he rolled away from the door and gestured me inside. "I know who you are. I watch your videos after all. Come on inside."

As I settled on a couch, he wheeled around to the other side of the coffee table before jerking a thumb back toward his kitchen. "Beer?" he asked. Declining the offer, I wondered where I should start. For a moment, a thick silence hung between us.

"So… is that from your service, or after?" I asked to break the silence, referring to his wheelchair. It may not be polite to talk about why someone was in a wheelchair for most of society, but vets tended to forgo caring about that kind of stuff around each other.

"Yeah, Persian Gulf War. I was shot in the leg multiple times," He said nonchalantly as if he talked about the weather. "What's your excuse?" His voice was gruff, but I knew he didn't mean anything by it. That's just how soldiers talked.

Chuckling at his phrasing, I shrugged. "Some kind of chemical bomb fucked up my lungs. They wouldn't let me stay on."

"That's rough," he replied. Smirking, he continued, "Anyway, now that the formalities are out of the way. I assume you have questions?"

"So many questions," I replied. "How long has it been since the VA first messed up your benefits?"

He made a show of counting on his fingers for a second before replying. "About eight years ago now, about. One day my wife just received a letter expressing condolences over the loss of her husband. If it weren't so infuriating, it would have been funny, considering I was sitting next to her at the time." He sighed and took a deep breath before continuing. "She's passed on now; God rest her soul. But back on track; they cut my benefits, my pension, my medical assistance, everything. Damn near killed me for real, considering I had no other source of income to feed myself."

"Are you still dealing with the fallout?" I asked.

He shook his head. "No, thank God. It took me a dozen calls and just about as many visits to the VA office to get them to admit that I was telling the truth, but they repealed everything eventually." Looking at me sympathetically, he continued, "Based on what I've seen from your videos, you're in a helluva lot more shit than me, though. My problems started and stopped with the VA. I never had to deal with any outside agencies."

I groaned internally. As excited as I had been to meet with someone else who had gone through the same thing as me, this visit was turning out to be a lot less fruitful than I'd hoped. There wasn't anything here I could use; no untapped knowledge about how to defeat the system that was trying so hard to defeat me. I couldn't tell Mr. Johnson that, though. "Yeah, I've got fraud investigators and government workers on my ass pretty much every day," I said instead. "Thank you for taking the time to see me, though. It helps a lot to get perspectives on other people who've gone through the same thing I have. Especially people who came out the other side intact."

"Well, as intact as I had been going in," he joked, rapping his knuckles on his wheelchair frame. We both chuckled. "I'm sorry I couldn't be any more direct help. My only advice? Don't give up. You're an army grunt, so I know you know that already, but just don't. And after this settles, come see me again. We'll crack open some cold ones and swap stories."

"I promise I won't, Mr. Johnson," I replied. "And it's a deal."

***

Life dragged on at a steady pace for a few weeks after that. Diana's support was the only thing that kept me going when there were long periods of no progress to my problems. My hand had finally healed, at least, which meant I could kill time by going back to work. On my way back from an evening shift one night in mid-February, one of my old buddies from the regiment called me to ask for a favor.

"What's up?" I asked as I tossed my keys on the kitchen counter and started digging through the fridge for a snack with my free hand.

"Rod, I need your help. I've been doing one-on-one training with this guy, you know, weight loss, fitness, the whole nine yards. Anyway, my sister is not doing so well so I have to fly out and see her. My problem is that if I put off this guy's sessions, he's going to slide backward on his progress. I know you're a fitness freak like me. Can you take over while I'm gone and keep this guy motivated?"

I understood the predicament. Falling off the wagon when it came to fitness was an easy way to lose months of hard work. However, I'd never trained anyone before, and I didn't even know where to start. I told my friend as much, but he brushed my hesitation aside.

"There's nothing to it, man. He isn't looking for some crazy special workout routines or anything. He just needs someone to put in the work next to him so that he feels obligated to stay committed. Can I count on you?"

Well, it's not like I've got a whole lot else going on right now, I thought. Besides, maybe I'd even end up enjoying myself. "Sure, man. Just text me the details for what I need to do," I said.

He gave me the guy's contact details, along with their current workout plan. Going on runs together every day became a new tradition. Fighting through my lung problems was a pain in the ass at first, but the longer we kept at it, the better I felt. I hadn't realized how much I missed exercising on this level. Ever since that first VA letter I'd been shirking my workouts and making excuses. Maybe this training regimen wasn't just good for keeping the client from falling off the wagon; it managed to get me back on, too. My friend had called me asking for a favor, but in the end, he'd ended up helping me more than I'd realized I needed. I'd have to thank him with a beer whenever he was back in town. I wrote a poem about this experience.

If you're going through Hell, keep going,
Regardless of the obstacles confronting you,
Never give up.
I'm certain.
You've experienced days where you are happy and smiling,
and days where you were sad or crying.
We've all had those times when we felt like we were taking four steps forward,
and then four steps back.
If today is one of those days,
Where think or feel that you're regressing, or,
You've not met your goals.
Listen to me.
Get up and never give up.
Why?
Because just remember,
You are not alone.
Millions of people across the world like me and you,

They experience triumphs and disappointments
You may feel like the disappointments are piling up
Think again because that's far from the truth.
Many around the globe,
at this moment are experiencing,
Unexplainable sicknesses,
living in poverty,
struggling with depression,
dealing with traumas
Or simply facing one trial after another.
So realize you're not alone suffering.
The nations survive not because of their power,
But because of its persistence.
This hope could not be told.
So push past the pain.
Fight for your goal,
Fight for life.

By the tenth day, I had managed to help the guy lose two sizes. His strength had improved significantly, too. I wasn't sure how long my friend had been working at his regimen before he'd handed it off to me, but I was surprised by the amount of progress I saw over such a short period of time.

"Push past the pain, you're halfway there, Josh!" I yelled encouragingly. "Come on, man! No point in turning back now! Finish it out!"

I felt like a boot instructor, except way nicer. "You came this far cause you can fucking do it!" Even as I screamed the words, I understood that I was also saying them to myself.

"Do it, Josh! You're not alone!" I shouted as we sprinted out our last quarter mile for the day. *I'm not alone, either.*

"You're a beast, Carmelo. I never thought I had this strength in me. Thanks, dude," Josh said one day after we'd wrapped up another intense session.

"If I ever hear that you quit after I stop being your instructor, I'll come and kick your ass, remember that," I warned jokingly.

"I think you'd be a badass fitness trainer," Diana commented, hovering over my shoulder as I edited the footage of the fitness journey for my vlog.

"You really think so?"

"Yeah! You're jacked, first of all," she said, laughing as I took a moment to pose and flex. "And you are awesome at motivational speaking as well," She added.

"Now you're just flattering me," I said in mock embarrassment.

Diana smiled and punched me on the arm playfully. "I'm serious! You just haven't really been paying attention to what you're accomplishing here. The response on your vlogs is a testament to what you're capable of."

Despite her insistence, I brushed Diana's appreciative comments off, assuming it was just another way for her to show me encouragement and affection.

When comments started pouring in on the video a week later, basically regurgitating what Diana said, I had to endure weeks of "I told you so."

The month came to an end with a fresh update to the Hell that was my reality. It was a Monday morning, and I was in the process of mentally gearing myself up to go to work when another letter came in. This particular letter took the form of a demand from the IRS that I supply them with my death certificate, which had apparently been sent to my previous address. I was at a loss for words. How could bureaucracy fuck up so badly that they could send a death certificate for someone who wasn't even dead to the wrong address, then send mail to the right address, demanding the death certificate back? It boggled the mind. As I stood in the middle of the living room, reading the letter over for a third time in an attempt to understand why I was being put through all of this shit, I heard Diana's voice from the doorframe to the bedroom.

"Another mail with bad news?" She asked.

I just nodded at her. No matter how hard I try to compose myself, it felt like one government entity or another always knew how to drag me back down.

"I just don't how much paperwork, applications, and proof I have to send to these people before they figure out that they made a mistake," I complained. "I'm almost convinced that they are doing it on purpose at this point."

Diana walked over and put an arm around my shoulder.

"You'll get through this. I know it's hard, but you will. We will," she assured me.

"I know, Babe," I said, sighing. "Don't worry about me. Get ready for work, I'm all right now." I kissed her tenderly and prepared breakfast for the both of us while she finished doing her hair. Somewhere between mixing pancake batter and pouring orange juice, I realized that Trisha would probably soon receive something similar from the IRS if she hadn't already. I decided to send her a quick text to avoid any awkward arguments or unnecessary drama later.

"Hey, just disregard the mail from IRS. I have received it and will deal with it accordingly. Say hi to Jaxon for me." I quickly typed in the message and hit the send button. I realized I had my work cut out for me this morning. First, I had to call the IRS to inform them of their mistake and give them a rundown of what had happened to me. At this point, I'd basically memorized the speech in a way that gave as much information as possible as clearly as possible. Yet still every government agency I talked to managed to get confused and failed to fix anything.

I paced the room as I dialed the IRS helpline and waited for my call to go through. Half an hour later, my patience was at its razor edge when I finally managed to connect. *Oh, you have got to be kidding me*, I thought when I was immediately put on hold. I'd spent all this time listening to the phone ringing and ringing and ringing, and now that they pick up, I get to hear elevator music. Where the fuck are the people that supposedly earn a paycheck working there?

The anger issues I had left behind years ago seemed to come flooding back. White-hot rage filled my veins. I wanted to break something. With a sweeping motion, I used my forearm to violently push an array of decorative glass jars and candles to the ground. The chaos of the crashed glasses gave me a momentary sense of satisfaction. My eyes fixated on the glass shards as I bent down and picked out one that looked sharper than all others. The cell phone tucked between my ear and my shoulder, I absentmindedly dragged the rough-edged glass shard on my wrist ever so slowly. I kept repeating the same movement thoughtlessly back and forth, back and forth. Dangerously close to the vein for no good reason. I was utterly numb to the world.

"Hello, my name is James. How can I help you today, sir?" came a monotone voice from the other end of the line. The recognizable script he followed gave me no hope that I'd find him helpful, but his voice did bring me back to my senses. The shocking realization of what I was trying to do horrified me as I stumbled backward, throwing the glass shard to the floor and shuddering in shock.

What the Hell was I even trying to attempt?

The representative cleared his throat to get my attention, "Sir, are you there?" he asked again.

"Um, yeah. I'm right here," I finally managed to form a coherent sentence.

"May I know your purpose for calling?" He asked, dryly.

"Yes, actually, I received a letter from IRS today demanding my death certificate, even though I'm alive and well. This is extra concerning because I've already previously notified the IRS of this mistake."

Despite the horror that my brain was processing, my voice held its usual professional quality over the phone. It was a strange, disjointed feeling to act like two separate people at the same time. One that was an emotional train wreck, and one that spent all his time making phone calls just like this one on autopilot.

After a predictable delay of shocked silence, the customer service agent attempted to recover his senses and asked me a series of questions to cross-check my identification. "Mr. Rodriguez, I'm forwarding you to the concerned department, kindly stay online," he said after I finished jumping through the usual hoops.

I rolled my eyes in response. *Why do they bother starting the conversation with, "How can I help you," if they never actually help anyone?*

I don't know if I was right or not, but I was losing hope in the system. I couldn't help but imagine a similar situation happening to a veteran who was in a more debilitating condition than me or one who didn't have access to even the meager resources I did to try to push back.

Another somber voice at the other end of the phone put a halt to my train of thoughts. As usual, I was forced to brief her on everything, despite having just done so with her subordinate. *If they can't communicate during the same*

160

phone call, no wonder they can't find their ass with two hands and fix me in their systems.

She asked me for the form number I had filled when I visited them.

Well, at least that's a new question, I thought, as I pulled my copy up from the folder of important documents I kept in my studio.

"Ok, sir, I see where the misunderstanding is. The investigator on your case transferred departments, and the investigation was stuck midway," she informed me in a calm tone.

"So, my case has just been sitting there in limbo?" *Just like me.* "What do I need do to get this fixed, then?" the irritation was visible in my tone.

"We shouldn't need anything else on your end. I will update your forms in the system, and the investigation for your case will be done promptly. We apologize for any inconvenience," she said.

"Wait a minute! What should I do in the meantime? I've been waiting for this investigation for months. My tax returns are stuck; my student loan isn't cleared..."

"...Sir, we can't expedite the investigation any faster than it already is. As far as clearing up confusion like this in the future, we are notified of a death by cross-agency data, specifically by the SSA. I urge you to get in touch with them to rectify," she said and ended the call before I could argue further.

"Like always," I muttered to myself. I looked at my bruised wrist and decided to apply some ointment, hoping that it wouldn't get any worse than it already seemed. I started sweeping up the mess I had created and contemplated my earlier actions.

It's probably best that Diana doesn't learn about this, I thought to myself as I piled the broken glass into a trash bag. A trip to Walmart and Ikea was in the pipeline since I had to replace the jars and candles before she got home. Given her detective skills, I wasn't sure I'd get away with it, but I had to try.

By the time she returned, everything was back in place, and a long sleeve shirt covered my bruised wrist. Dinner passed uneventfully, and we got ready for bed shortly after. As we hit the mattress, Diana passed out almost instantly while I stayed wide awake. Staring at her peaceful, slumbering face, I wanted to kick myself for what I had debated attempting. Before all of this, I had never been suicidal, fucked up, sure. Self-destructive? Check. However, I'd never gotten this deep down the rabbit hole before. Lack of sleep, constant depression, and stress were taking a toll on me. I could feel myself slowly fading from inside. I wanted a way out of this mess.

***

"The new semester is about to start," I told Diana as we went for a boat ride the following weekend. It had been a while since we'd spent any quality time together, given our jobs.

"I hope they sort out your loan issues soon," she commented. I looked out at the wide horizon of the harbor and wondered what the future held for me. It had been almost five months since I was declared dead by the US government, but I was still dealing with weekly encounters from investigators.

Five long months of despair, disappointment, and an aversion to ever rechecking my mailbox, sulking about it on this trip would be a waste. I tried to cheer myself up for Diana's sake. Whipping out my camera, I filmed some footage of our boat ride. My vlogs were not just about the dead man's case updates. That was the bread and butter, sure, but slowly and steadily, I was showcasing my life. I needed to tell the world what I was fighting for, along with what I was fighting against.

The next couple of days, my phone rang constantly. Ever since I'd jump-started the stalled investigation with the IRS, I was getting contacted day and night by people trying to verify my identity. They'd always have a long list of questions, and when I answered them to a tee, they always seemed surprised. In their eyes, I had to be some case of identity fraud. The real reason was too fantastical, too unbelievable for them to accept. None of them ever apologized for their suspicion, however. That had started to grate on me more and more as time passed. My honor and my integrity were continually being called into question, and no one seemed to care about how that made me feel. However, no matter how they treated me, I would prove them wrong. I would get my identity back.

"Babe, I think you could even answer those questions in your sleep," Diana teased when I hung up the phone on another investigator that had called in the middle of dinner.

"I wonder if that's a marketable skill," I joked back. Life sucked, but that didn't give me an excuse to mope the entire time. If I couldn't always be happy for my own sake, the least I could do is try to keep up appearances for Diana.

Recording and editing booth.

CHAPTER 12

I was trying not to raise my voice, but it echoed anyway, inside the small office where I was meeting with my VA advocate. "Can you please help me find a lawyer who knows anything about a situation like mine? I have reached out to dozens of them, and no one has experience in this particular situation. They keep recommending other lawyers hoping they could help instead. I'm tired of being passed off like some shitty appliance that gets re-gifted every year."

"I feel for you, Mr. Rodriguez. We can try to assist you with that, but our advocacy program is designed to help you as a veteran interact with the VA as an entity. Our ability to act on your behalf outside of that scope is limited."

I'd heard it before. My direct issue with the VA, my benefits, and my pension had already been resolved. So, I was basically being told that there was nothing left for the VA to do to help me. I thanked the advocate for her insight and left the building feeling dejected. I wasn't sure why I thought that going back and meeting with them would help. I needed to be meeting with the IRS, the SSA, and just about everyone else, but the VA was, ironically, no longer on my list of priorities at this point.

My next vlog followed the depressing mood that had been hanging over me from my meeting. I shared what the advocate had said about their inability to help, and practically pleaded with my audience to send lawyers my way if they knew anyone. It wasn't a proud moment for me, but I didn't know how else to ask for help anymore. A few hours after the update went live, and my phone rang. Checking the caller ID, it listed the caller as blocked.

In my experience, the only kind of people who block their number were prank callers and people who don't mean you well. So, I left it to ring, opting to start preparing dinner instead. Half an hour later, it rang again. The same blocked number stared up at me from the screen. Again, I ignored it.

"Persistent fucker aren't you," I said out loud when it began ringing a third time. Picking my phone up, I decided to answer. It would probably end up being just another investigator.

"Am I speaking with Mr. Carmelo Rodriguez?" a deep, masculine voice said.

"You are, yes. May I ask whom I'm speaking with?" I replied.

"My name is not a concern. I'd like to stay anonymous."

I was taken aback by his demand. Why would anyone ask not to reveal their identity? This felt like the kind of thing you saw and movies and said *That's so unrealistic. Nobody talks like that.* However, here I was, on the phone with God knows who, getting toyed around with once again. I was not in the mood.

"Is it some sort of a prank? Dude, I am so not in the mind frame to deal with this shit. Waste someone else's time," I said, disconnecting the call before the mystery man could reply. As if there wasn't enough on my plate to deal with, I hadn't even put my phone down when it rang again. *Blocked number*. Rejecting the call, I tried to go back to my cooking, but it buzzed again, and again. Fighting the urge to throw my phone against a wall, I picked up. "I've already told you that I'm not interested in whatever anonymous games you are playing. Don't test my patience. Why are you calling me and how the Hell do you know my name?" I demanded as my nostrils flared with anger.

"If you'd just practice a bit of patience and listen to me, you'll understand that I'm not wasting your time," the voice said. "I completely understand your agitation, Mr. Rodriguez. Five months is a long time to keep fighting with the system. Especially without any help or assistance."

Well, that answers one question, I thought. Or at least, I assumed it did. "So you know me from my *YouTube* channel," I said.

"From the very first video that you uploaded," he replied curtly.

"Okay?" He seemed to want a specific response, but I did not know what else to say or what to expect.

"The very first video that was pulled off the internet," he reiterated, specifying the event where my first upload had unexpectedly gone offline for a few hours. "Have you ever wondered why it was taken down?"

"Honestly? Right when it was happening, sure, but I assumed that I'd tripped an automated copyright strike or something and they put it back up when it got manually reviewed." I offered the only plausible explanation I had.

"Let me confirm one thing, Mr. Rodriguez. I went through your video frame by frame, and I couldn't even find something that could reasonably trigger a false positive," he explained. "You, my friend, are not being treated fairly."

The way he said that made it sound like there was more going on here than there first appeared. Intrigued, I said, "All right, I'm interested in hearing what you have to say."

"We'll start with a small introduction. I prioritize my safety, but I understand that to gain trust, sometimes one must give trust. Let's say I'm a lawyer by profession, and I've been following your case from its inception. I think I can help you…"

"…You're a lawyer? Are you willing to represent me?" Interrupting him mid-sentence.

"I cannot represent you, but I can provide you with information that you will find useful. Grab something to write with; I'm only going to go over all of this once."

Fishing through our junk drawer in the kitchen, I managed to find an old Christmas card with a blank back and a crayon that Jaxon had left behind on his last visit. "All right," I said. "I'm ready."

"First things first, from today onward, you'll have to reign in that temper of yours. Other people who can help you might call and not all of them will be as patient as I was."

My brow furrowed as I almost snapped back at him before realizing that was precisely the sort of behavior he was talking about. Rolling my neck instead, I simply continued to listen.

"Good, I see you're a quick learner," the lawyer said. It was creepy that he seemed to be able to read my reaction so accurately through the phone. "The second thing you need to write down is that you will start receiving offers from

168

people who can offer you and your cause exposure. Take it. I know you are a busy man, but if you want your life back, you need to make this your first priority. For example, I know that you still have not found the time to reply to every news outlet that has emailed you."

His accurate information both confused and stung. How did he know that? It wasn't my fault; most of those media outlets wanted me to trash talk the government or promote their bias instead of just getting word about my problem out. Being able to sift through the trash to find the respectable outlets took time.

"Third," the voice continued, "I'm going to give you a list of contacts that you will have to reach out to." He proceeded to list a series of names, sometimes associating them with phone numbers or emails, and other times with strangely specific details on what to say to them.

"Now, making use of those things will help generate controversy around your plight. Have you ever considered filing a suit against the VA or the SSA for causing damages to your wellbeing and livelihood?" he asked.

"My girlfriend and I discussed it once in passing, but I've never given it any real serious thought," I replied.

"You should. Pressuring them with court action will rattle them a bit and will motivate those with the power actually to get things done and to pay attention to you. As opposed to the underlings you deal with every week right now. I already said I could not represent you, but I will give you a list of attorneys who probably can. Be warned that while all of them have the necessary knowledge to take your case, not all of them will be easily convinced to help."

"Even just knowing that people with that kind of expertise exist is a morale booster," I assured him as I scribbled out the second list of names. "If all of this works, I owe you my life. How can I ever repay you?"

"Don't worry about repaying me," the voice said. "Just continue putting the word out there any way you can. Being in your position is difficult, and if you can help others with the information, I'm using to help you, then you can consider the net positive force we put out into the universe as my repayment. We will probably never speak again, but I will continue to follow your case through your vlogs. Good luck, Mr. Rodriguez."

And with that, he hung up the phone. *What in the actual fuck just happened,* I thought to myself? Staring down at the hastily scrawled abundance of information that I'd been fed, I wondered if any of it would prove useful. *Only one way to find out.* The first thing the next morning, I'd start giving that list of lawyers a call.

The next day, my resolve to start contacting lawyers was interrupted by a wave of fresh support on my *Facebook* and other social media handles. Someone with many followers had shared a link to my series, and I was getting double the traffic I had been in recent weeks. My inbox was overflowing with messages of support and love. Among the many messages, one stood out -- an invite from a veteran's support group who wanted me to speak at the veteran's retreat event in NYC in the upcoming week.

I dropped them my number to discuss further details about it and then decided that before I started calling lawyers, I should *Google* what it takes to sue government agencies. The mystery man had told me not every lawyer would be easily convinced to take my case, and I thought that the more I knew about my situation going in, the easier it would be to persuade them to take me on as a client.

While all of this was going on, I continually received reminders from my college with requests to clear the payment to continue pursuing my education. Since the IRS had not yet resolved my student loan problem, I had to personally request an exception from the dean to keep me enrolled at the very last minute. Thankfully, he granted it without any issues.

Now armed with the internet's knowledge on suing the government, it was almost dark when Diana entered the apartment to find me knee-deep in a pile of paperwork and forms that I printed. I needed all of the papers to my left, right and center to initiate the lawsuit.

"All those poor trees," Diana said, staring at the vast amounts of paper.

"Our poor printer ink is more like it," I replied jokingly before adding in a more serious tone. "Bringing a lawsuit against government agencies is a complicated process."

"I believe in you, Babe," she kissed me on the forehead before trying to navigate her way to the kitchen. "Let's have dinner, and then I'll let you get back to your justice via paperwork."

I couldn't help but grin at her need to make food a priority. Agreeing to a break, I stood and stretched my arms. This time tomorrow, I planned to have everything I needed to file my suit.

"Mr. Rodriguez, I'm highly impressed with your preparation and planning, but this is a case that could take years and years in the courts. You have to understand that in the end, the result might still not be to your satisfaction."

One of the attorneys told me as he declined my case. Over the course of next week, I called every lawyer on the list that the mystery man had given me. Every single one of them sympathized with my situation and applauded my resolve, but none of them agreed to take my case. I knew that he'd warned me that this might happen, but it was still disappointing. That was when I remembered something else, he said.

"It is possible that waiting to find a suitable attorney might hinder your lawsuit plans. In that case, remember not to waste any more time and file the claim yourself. This will bring attorneys interested in hunting high profile cases right to you, rather than the other way around."

One quick stop to the nearest Staples for an excessive amount of envelopes, later I sent off every form and file that I needed to start my claim. *It feels good to be the one sending the shitty-to-receive mail for once*, I thought to myself with a snicker.

On my way back up the stairs, my phone lit up with the veteran's retreat program that had messaged me.

"Mr. Rodriguez, we want you to speak at our event about your story to create awareness among the audience. Many seasoned veterans will be there to speak as well, but we are particularly interested in hearing what you have to say," the man said over the phone.

"I would love to be a part of it. Mail me everything you want me to cover, and we'll continue from there."

"Thank you so much, sir. You have no idea how much I admire you. I am a regular follower of your vlogs," he replied.

I thanked him for his kind words and ended the call with a promise to look at their details as soon as they sent them.

The veteran's retreat was scheduled for a week later. A couple of days before I was due to give my speech, news of my lawsuit broke on a couple of news sites and the internet. All of the agencies I had filed against had declined to comment, but the event itself had still caused quite a stir.

Morning until evening my phone buzzed with news reporters questioning my motives and asking for details about the case. A very famous journalist on national television reached out to me after following the lawsuit. They wanted to do a whole segment on me, which I agreed to. Everything was happening so fast that I had no idea how to feel about it.

The point of the veteran's retreat was just that; it was a retreat. Its primary purpose was to be relaxing; a getaway for those who attended. However, I hoped that my speech, despite its serious topic, would be a positive influence over the event.

"Before we kick start this wonderful retreat, I want to applaud all you veterans who came today in support. I would like to invite a very special guest in front who has been crashing the news this whole week. Carmelo Rodriguez is our esteemed speaker for the day. Let's give him a warm welcome, ladies, and gentlemen."

The host introduced me as light applause rippled from the audience who greeted me.

I cleared my throat. I'd been practicing this speech all week, but I still had to cross my fingers that I did not choke over what I was about to say. I began my speech.

"Hello, friends. I will try my best not to bore you with long stories, but instead focus on something that you can all resonate with too. So, please bear with me while I share my story. My name is Carmelo Rodriguez. I used to be a decorated war soldier, but my career was cut short after the chemical toxins from a bomb blast on the battlefield invaded my bloodstream and completely destroyed my immune system. Long story short, I did not lose myself to the bullets and bombs, but I still lost my ability to serve. It took months and years to come to terms with the truth…"

"...Thank you for your service. I hear this every veteran's day to be reminded of what I lost. Being a part of this military was my one true passion. I wanted to die, but I decided that was cowardly and so, I learned to live. I decided to live and make a life for me here in this city. I became a student, I worked hard to reintegrate with society like everyone else and I survived. I survived the guns, the bullets, the bombs. Heck, I even survived grocery and examinations. Then one day all of a sudden, the agencies that looked after citizen's rights declared me dead. Six months from then I've been fighting to prove I am not a fraud and I am alive and well. The label of a dead man haunts me every day. I've punished and tortured myself over it. I've lost my patience and trust in the system. But that day I decided I will not take my life. I will not be among the twenty-two veterans who give up their lives every day. I decided I will stand up for myself and others like me so the agencies would not mess with our sanity ever again. We came from war-torn areas shattered and broken beyond repair. The demons haunt us every night and we adjust to live with them. Venlafaxine, Sertralin, Prazosin, topped with Doxepin, I'm sure most of you have heard of this cocktail. The mental health is real, we are not a broken mess. We've been fighters on the field and off the field as well. So I urge you all today to never give up. No matter how hard it gets, take charge of your lives. Be proud of yourselves that you've served your country well and don't let guilt or depression get. Reach out for help. Because there is no shame in doing. As for me, I will get my life back."

That speech marked my first standing ovation. I thought I'd felt a rush when I'd delivered my poem back at Penn State, but that was nothing compared to this. My heart swelled with pride and joy and determination as I looked out on the crowd of veterans just like me. Saying all that in front of so many people wasn't easy, but I knew I had the chance to say something fundamental and have it be heard.

The ordeal of being a dead man showed me one positive aspect of me which was that I still had the fight and passion for achieving my goals. I wasn't giving up, and I wasn't ready to back down from a good fight. My training as a soldier was still there; unwavering and unbent resolve was my superpower.

Almost fifteen days after filing by my claim, I started getting the calls I had been anxiously waiting to receive. Lawyers from the VA, IRS, SSI and many other agencies began reaching out, trying to gauge how serious I was and whether they could cut a deal and settle.

"We deeply regret the frustration this must have caused you, Mr. Rodriguez. Please get back to me as soon as you can, so we sort this issue somehow."

Messages like these filled in my inbox, and I was thrilled that we were finally getting somewhere since I was ready to cooperate fully. I had never been in it for the money, and if I could get them to give me my life back, I was more than willing to let them save face in return.

A week later, Diana brought in a piece of mail as she came back from work. "Babe, you have a letter from the IRS," she called out for me.

"Oh my god, what is it now?" I groaned while ripping the envelope open. Staring at the paper for a moment, I lost my ability to react.

"Bad news?" Diana asked, ready to hear the new way that they'd decided to screw me over.

"No!" I smiled, holding it up for her to see. "No. They sorted out my tax returns!"

"That's great! If they're working on that, that means they'll probably get to your student loans soon, too, right?"

"That's what I'm hoping," I admitted. "Then, I can pay for school and get back on track with my MBA!"

Things were finally moving forward on every front. I still had much work to do, but it felt like I was on the offensive finally, and that felt good. My story broke on *Channel 11 News*, where the host covered my story and what I was going through.

I was no longer afraid of the letters in my mailbox. The VA responded to my claim and assigned me an investigator for my lawsuit.

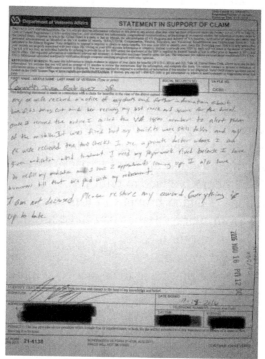

Tort claim made by Carmelo.

"Finally, we're getting somewhere with my claim. The red flags from the IRS are pretty much resolved which means I can start working with my supervisors to go back next semester at all costs. I'm committed to continuing living my life to the fullest and with a positive outlook. Never give up," I said into the camera.

Two days later, I received another letter from the Social Security Association and other updates started to come in too fast for me to keep the vlog current.

"Diana! Where are you, Babe?" I screamed into the phone.

"I'm on the way, honey. What is it?" She asked, alarmed.

"The SSA declared me alive. I just received a letter." I panted for breath.

All I heard in return was a high-pitched scream of excitement. "I'll be there as soon as possible," she said once she'd finished emptying her lungs. "We're celebrating tonight."

I sank on the couch again with tears flowing as I reread the letter, and again. The SSA office apologized for the harm they'd caused me for disseminating the records of my death. They only explanation they offered was that the SSA department got their information from the hospital records where my name, date of birth, and social security number were listed under deceased veterans. According to them, it was their obligation to inform other agencies of the information that was relegated to them with other governmental institutions and agencies.

As I got a hold of my emotions, I skimmed the other information and instructions, which stated that I was supposed to send a copy of this letter to all the agencies who declared me deceased and also keep a copy safe for future use if the need arises in an unfortunate case. Unable to contain my excitement and nervous energy, I took to my studio to record my victory vlog before Diana got home. This video was so much different from the other ones.

I could finally see myself being happy in front of the camera as I said, "The tag of a dead man is off my shoulder. I can finally feel alive. I don't feel like a remnant of a decaying corpse. The government is no longer burying me in deep pity called grave. I can learn, I can try things I have always wanted to. I will inspire those around me. I will do the things that I love; I will do them with those whom I love. I will soar through the sky. And I will reach new heights. Because as of yet, I am not dead."

As I wrapped up the raw recording, I heard Diana's hasty footsteps through the doorway. She called out for me, and her voice radiated the same happiness that I felt pulsing through my core.

Opening the front door, she didn't bother kicking off her shoes as she charged right for me. She flew right into my arms with tears glimmering in her eyes. I held her in my and gave her a spin. We were both hysterically laughing and crying at the same time. After a few minutes, we calmed down and sat beside each other, panting heavily, but still beaming from ear to ear.

"So it's finally behind us. It's over," she whispered.

"It is finally over," I repeated. "Can you believe it? It took almost a year for them to conclude that I was alive."

"So, you are officially alive now?" Diana started laughing again.

"Until a meteor hits this apartment or other further notice, yeah. I'm actually officially alive. I chuckled and then winced as she threw a series of cushions at me.

"If you ever say something like this ever again, I kill you with my own hands," she warned me.

"Let's go out tonight and just let loose," I decided.

"We will celebrate to the fullest tonight," Diana agreed.

That night we drank and danced like there was no tomorrow.

"I was afraid that it might never end for me, and I will have to suffer from this for the rest of my life," I admitted, feeling vulnerable as we danced to a slow tune.

"I know. Sometimes I would get worried for you. You had become so destructive. I tried to ignore it since I knew you needed the space," she confided in return.

"What will happen to the lawsuit? Are you still going to follow through now that you're alive?" Diana asked again.

"Yeah, the attorney said we should take anyone who didn't try to settle with me to court. Both for reparations for us, but also to help set a precedent that might help others in the future," I replied.

"So this was just the first victory. There's more left to the journey," she said.

"There's always more to the journey," I said. "But I can weather any storm and walk any distance as long as I can do it with you at my side."

"You are such a romantic soul. I am so happy to see you finally not in your brooding dark mood," she kissed me, and we wrapped our hands around each other while we swayed to the music.

***

One year later…

I woke up to the bright sun peeking through the windows since Diana as always deliberately left the curtains open.

"She'll never stop hating to watch me sleep more than her," I groaned. She was now training for induction as a

179

pilot in the US Air force, which had her leaving bright and early every morning much to her chagrin.

The only thing that was stuck since last year was the lawsuit that did not seem to have an ending in sight. A high-profile attorney approached me about taking the case, just like the mystery voiced man had told me someone would. I still thought about that phone call often wondering who that man had been, what his motives were, and how I could ever let him know how thankful I was.

The best I could do, I decided, was to go to court. Push the fight that he'd encouraged me to push and continue to document the whole thing for others to watch and hopefully learn from my experience.

***

Clad in a crisply pressed blue suit, I waited patiently to be invited inside. Today was the day of my resurrection. Before I could enter the courtroom, I sat in the corridor, letting wave after wave of impending doom wash over me trying to erode my resolve and months of preparation.

I sat back against the wall, head down. I looked at my wristwatch, *still, ten minutes until the hearing.*

The words of my drill sergeant pervaded my thoughts, *'If you're ten minutes early, you're on time, if you're on time, you're late.'* I'm not sure what being thirty minutes early means, but there I was.

A stranger's voice broke through my spiraling thoughts and yanked me back to the court hallway, "Hey, man. I've seen you somewhere. Are you famous or something?"

My eyes shot up to see a janitor eyeing me inquisitively. I straightened my posture so I wouldn't look as defeated. His eyes widened in realization once he saw my face.

"Oh, Oh, you're..." he paused, unsure how to broach this sensitive subject.

I decided to make it easier for him. "Yes, I am the dead vet."

He smiled warmly or sympathetically, like he wanted to extend his support but did not know what to say; he managed an awkward, "all right," then hurried away mopping the floor.

This was the usual reaction, an awkward silence, a benign expression, a figurative pat on the shoulder. I suppose I can't blame them. No one knows how to act around the dead.

My wristwatch beeped, the final alarm signaling that it was time to begin.

ABOUT THE AUTHOR

Carmelo Rodriguez is an author, a veteran, and a father who learned early in his life, that life is never easy. When an error by the Veterans Administration declared him 'Dead,' he lost all of his benefits and found himself in a battle with the US Government bombarded with bureaucracy and repercussions. Agency after agency followed suit and declared him dead as well sending him into a spiraling effort to claim his identity and to be reported alive. To bring light to his case and to help others who may be going through the same thing, he started a Vlog, which ultimately gained him national attention. He fights for justice for other veterans and finds the time to feed the homeless. Rodriguez lives with Diana in DC and currently works as a police officer.

FOLLOW CARMELO ON HIS BLOG AND SOCIAL MEDIA

https://www.carmelorodriguez-author.com/
https://www.facebook.com/VetDocSeriesCEO/

DEAD SOLDIER

Made in the USA
Middletown, DE
01 December 2020